[ BLANK ]

Alice Birch

# [ BLANK ]

*methuen* | drama

LONDON · NEW YORK · OXFORD · NEW DELHI · SYDNEY

METHUEN DRAMA

Bloomsbury Publishing Plc, 50 Bedford Square, London, WC1B 3DP, UK
Bloomsbury Publishing Inc, 1385 Broadway, New York, NY 10018, USA
Bloomsbury Publishing Ireland, 29 Earlsfort Terrace, Dublin 2, D02 AY28, Ireland

BLOOMSBURY, METHUEN DRAMA and the Methuen Drama logo
are trademarks of Bloomsbury Publishing Plc

First published in Great Britain by Oberon Books 2019
This edition published by Methuen Drama 2022
Reprinted 2022, 2023, 2024, 2025

*Thanks to:*

Ayesha, Shona, Sophia, Jackie, Grace, Lucy, Zaris-Angel,
Zainab, Jo, Thusita, Petra, Leah, Kate, Ashna,
Jemima & Taya

Maria Aberg, Rosie Elnile, Jess Bernberg,
Carolyn Downing, Heta Multanen, Ayse Tashkiran,
Cat Beveridge, Diane Willmott-Stiles, Suzanne Bourke,
Amy Bending, Aimee Wood, Sydney Florence,
Ryan O'conner and Blythe Stewart

Róisín McBrinn, Lucy Perman, Michael Longhurst,
Clare Slater, Anna Cooper, Lucy Morrison, Mimi Findlay,
Charlotte Gwinner, Phyllida Lloyd and Tom Lyons

Everyone at the Donmar, Clean Break and NT Connections

Giles, Geoff, Rachel, Jen, Sam and Arthur

*[BLANK]* was first co-commissioned by Clean Break and the National Theatre and a version was produced as part of NT Connections in 2018.

This production, a co-production between the Donmar Warehouse and Clean Break, began at the Donmar Warehouse on 11 October 2019 with the following cast in alphabetical order:

AYESHA ANTOINE
SHONA BABAYEMI
SOPHIA BROWN
JACKIE CLUNE
GRACE DOHERTY
LUCY EDKINS
ZAINAB HASAN
ZARIS-ANGEL HATOR
JOANNA HORTON
THUSITHA JAYASUNDERA
PETRA LETANG
LEAH MONDESIR-SIMMONDS
KATE O'FLYNN
ASHNA RABHERU
JEMIMA ROOPER
TAYA TOWER

| | |
|---|---|
| *Director* | Maria Aberg |
| *Designer* | Rosie Elnile |
| *Lighting Designer* | Jess Bernberg |
| *Sound Designer* | Carolyn Downing |
| *Movement Director* | Ayse Tashkiran |
| *Video Designer* | Heta Multanen |
| *Musical Director* | Cat Beveridge |
| *Fight Director* | Rachel Bown-Williams |
| | Of RC-Annie Ltd |
| *Casting Director* | Anna Cooper CDG |
| *Production Manager* | Diane Willmott-Stiles |
| *Company Stage Manager* | Suzanne Bourke |
| *Deputy Stage Manager* | Amy Bending |
| *Assistant Stage Manager* | Aimee Woods |
| *Costume Supervisor* | Sydney Florence |
| *Props Supervisor* | Lisa Buckley |
| | & Ryan O'Conner |
| *Dialect Coach* | Hazel Holder |
| *Resident Assistant Director* | Blythe Stewart |
| *Rehearsal And* | |
| *Production Photography* | Helen Maybanks |

**THE DONMAR WAREHOUSE** is a 251-seat, not-for-profit theatre in Covent Garden, led by Artistic Director Michael Longhurst and Executive Director Henny Finch. We have won more than 100 awards in our 27-year history.

We bring together a wide variety of people at our intimate warehouse space and elsewhere to create, witness and participate in thrilling, world-class theatre.

Through our work on and offstage, we aim to create a more cohesive, functional and creative society by broadening horizons, inspiring empathy and offering outstanding entertainment.

We develop new artists and future audiences through our renowned training programmes and our Discover activity with schools and communities.

We believe that representation matters; diversity of identity, of perspective, of lived experience enriches our work and our lives.

Welcome to important stories, thrillingly told, widely shared.

Find out more at
www.donmarwarehouse.com

**FORTY YEARS OF CHANGING LIVES AND MINDS**

## WHO WE ARE

Clean Break is a women's theatre company established by two women prisoners in 1979 at HMP Askham Grange in Yorkshire. For forty years we have used theatre to transform the lives of women with criminal justice experience and audiences' minds with ground-breaking theatre.

## WHAT WE DO

Our award-winning theatre productions share the often-hidden stories of women and crime with audiences. We are proud to have co-produced our new plays with dozens of UK theatres, including the Royal Court Theatre, Manchester Royal Exchange, Birmingham Rep, Theatr Clwyd, The Royal Shakespeare Company and Soho Theatre.

We have engaged with thousands of women on the fringes or with experience of the criminal justice system (our Members) from our women-only building in Kentish Town - a safe space where learning happens, and transformation becomes possible. The programme's success has grown generations of highly skilled and confident alumni, 70% of whom currently progress to further studies, employment or longer-term volunteering.

> *"It was a breath of fresh air; it took me out of here and helped me to imagine something better."* Participant at HMP Low Newton

Clean Break has been fortunate to work with many extraordinary writers and creative teams over the past forty years. Our commissioning process offers a unique exchange between artists, our Members and women in prison. Many of the artists we work with cherish their time with Clean Break and have been articulate about how formative their time with us has been.

> *"As a young female playwright, lots of the texts I was picking up were commissioned by Clean Break. And often the plays felt quite quiet; it wasn't about women walking into places and shooting everybody, it wasn't highly glamorised. I really felt drawn to the quiet craft, the kindness."* Alice Birch on writing for Clean Break, 2019

## SUPPORT US

We can't do what we do without you. If you'd like to help us use theatre to change lives, please visit our website, www.cleanbreak.org.uk.

Clean Break would like to acknowledge the generosity of all its funders and supporters. In particular, Arts Council England, The Lovington Foundation, Backstage Trust, Diana Ross, Baroness Simone Finn, The Baroness Kidron OBE and Dame Harriet Walter DBE.

## KEEP IN TOUCH

Be first in the know for all Clean Break's news by signing up to our newsletter via our website, or follow us on our social media channels:

Twitter: @CleanBrk | Facebook: /cleanbreak | Instagram: @CleanBrk

Clean Break, 2 Patshull Road, London NW5 2LB
020 7482 8600 | general@cleanbreak.org.uk | www.cleanbreak.org.uk

Registered company number 2690758 | Registered charity number 1017560

Supported using public funding by
**ARTS COUNCIL
ENGLAND**

This play is a challenge and an invitation to you and your company to make your own play from these scenes. This play might have a narrative and recurring characters, or it might not – it is entirely up to you.

The rules below are to help you complete this.

The play consists of 100 scenes in total.
Scenes 1 – 45 are for children.
Scenes 46 – 55 are for adults and children.
Scenes 56 – 100 are for adults.

The word 'children' has been used for differentiation and clarity. Children includes aged 18 and under. Adult includes 18 and over.

You and your company can choose as many or as few scenes as you like.

You may present them in any order you like. You may repeat scenes.

Gender specific pronouns and words such as 'she' 'he' 'they' Mum' 'daughter' 'son' 'Dad' 'wife' 'Aunt' 'Uncle' 'husband' 'sister' 'brother' etc. can and ought to be changed in order to construct your own narratives.

Where a name should be used, I have put the letter. If the characters are talking about somebody who is *not* in that scene then I have used 'NAME1 / NAME2 / NAME3'. Your company ought to choose names to insert here, and can use this to help construct narratives and recurring characters if you wish.

Letters (A / B etc.) denote a change of speaker in each scene - you shouldn't assume that 'A' in Scene One is the same speaker as 'A' in Scene Two etc. You can and ought to replace these letters with character names to construct (or not) your own through lines.

The play is performable without any set and any props. No prop mentioned within the dialogue is necessary.

/ Denotes the overlapping of speech. Words in square brackets [ ] are not spoken. The absence of a full stop at the end of a line denotes a kind of interruption – the lines should run at speed. The use of a full stop on a line on its own suggests a pause – whether this is a single beat or ten minutes depends on what feels right.

The spacing of the dialogue, the use of upper and lower case letters and the punctuation is all there to help the actor in terms of the pacing and the weight of their words.

# Children Scenes.

## 1. RYEVITA.

**This scene is between two children (A and B).**

A: Mum

B: Nope.

A: .

Where is

B: Don't know.

A: .

Have you not seen

B: Nope.

A: .

Has she

B: Nope.

.

A: What's that

B: Food

A: Not that

B: Ryevita to be

A: Not that

B: precise – how can you tell when Ryevita has gone off?

A: Not the

B: Tastes like wallpaper – is that just how it / tastes

A: / Not the fucking Ryevita

B: S'rank. And Bizarre – have you ever seen her eat a Ryevita in your

A: Not that I'm not asking about the fucking Ryevita what the fuck is that

B: That

A: Yes

B: This

A: Jesus Christ, I swear to fucking -

B: Drink

A: Can see it's fucking

B: Why d'you ask then

A: Cos I'm a little bit

B: What

A: Little bit fucking shocked to be honest

B: Right

A: That you're

B: Right

A: And

B: Right

A: Being so fucking Casual about

B: Right

A: So fucking Blatant about

B: You'd like me to drink in a Different manner

A: Fucking

B: Less Casual and Not Blatant?

.

 Literally no idea what that would look like

A: Seriously you are fucking

B: Did you learn to swear while you were gone

A: Fucking necking

B: Is that where you've Been?

A: Just

B: At Swear School

A: This is fucking outrageous

B: There Are Other ones 'A'

A: What even Is

B: There are other really Good swear words available to you
   if you want to stretch

A: Is that Archers

B: Stretch your vocabulary a bit

A: Is that Shitting Archers

B: That's very impressive

A: Are you drinking it Neat

B: What you did just then – Shitting – that's very Original

A: Seriously, are you drinking Neat Archers

B: The taps aren't running

A: You were planning on having it with Water

B: Does any of this look Planned?

A: You're fucking nuts

B: Does this look like a situation I have been Planning?

A: Cracked – you're cracked

B: It's all gone

A: What's all gone

B: The fucking food the fucking water the fucking electricity
has all fucking gone and she has gone She has gone she
has Definitely Gone this time and you were gone you
were gone for three days and I was Scared I was Properly
Scared.

You SHIT.

There is literally nothing left in the fridge or the cupboard
or underneath the fridge or round the back of the
cupboards or in the freezer or round the back of the
freezer or under the floorboards or in the garden – there is
Nothing in the garden – you know that stuff you thought
was chives – well it's fucking Not – there is nothing
growing in the garden there is nothing in the soil and I
went really deep – there is nothing all along the fences
and there is nothing underneath the fences and there is
nothing in the garden next door or the one next to that
and there is nothing in the bins I have literally licked
them clean so after this Ryevita – this Ryevita that I have
been holding onto til I thought I didn't have a choice, this
Ryevita is the Only In Emergencies Okay – after This has
gone there is literally nothing left and I am not using the
word Literally for effect or emphasis or like a dickhead

here but because it is the most accurate and specific and Correct word for the situation – she has never been gone this long before and I think we are a little bit fucked.

.

A: Why're you under the table?

B: You don't say Neat by the way. You don't roll your glass across the bar and say I'll have an Archers. Neat.

A: 'B'.

Why're you under the table?

B: Gimme an Archers. On the rocks.

A: 'B'.

Come on.

B: WKD. With a twist.

A: I'm sorry, alright. I am really profoundly sorry.

.

B: I nearly ate next door's rabbit.

A: .

B: I am not fucking kidding.

A: 'B'.

Come out from under there.

.

B: D'you want some?

.

A: She's coming back.

B: Earthquakes.

A: 'B'

B: .

A: She is. I know she is. She always does.

.

B: Not literally. Not actually Earthquakes. Just. Felt like one. Just really really felt like one.

It's warmer under here. My fingers are blue. Look.

## 2. WORK.

**This scene is between two children (A and B), or one Adult (A) and one child (B). A should always be older than B.**

B: Where's Mum again

A: At work

B: That's right

A: Yep

B: Special kind of work

A: That's it

B: Work

A: Yes.

B: .

A: .

B: Work where she doesn't come home

A: That's right.

B: Cos she has to sleep there.

A: That's it.

B: Sort of like Boarding School but for Work

A: Yes exactly

B: And not for kids, but for adults

A: Yes

B: And not for rich people.

A: Well.

It's Work isn't it.

B: And rich people don't work.

A: Sometimes that's true.

B: .

A: .

B: D'you reckon she'll be at this one for long?

A: Probably.

It's a good job.

B: Right.

A: She doesn't like not seeing you

B: No

A: But it's a job

B: Yes

A: Important

B: Right

A: Not that you're Not important

B: Okay

A: You're Very important

B: Right

A: The Most important

B: Okay

A: But this is Work

B: Right.

Work.

A: .

B: .

A: You're not eating.

B: .

A: What's wrong?

B: Can't eat fish fingers.

A: Oh.

You didn't say

B: I didn't want you to be upset

A: I'm not upset

B: She gets upset

A: Yes

B: When she's at work

A: Yes

B: But it's just work

A: Yes

B: That's where she is

A: Yep

B: I guess some people just get upset at their place of work

A: I guess so

B: She was crying

A: Yes

B: On the phone earlier, she kept crying

A: It will get easier for both of you

B: Once she settles in at work

A: Exactly

B: Makes friends and stuff

A: Yes

B: Starts earning shitloads of money.

Company car.

Work trips and stuff.

You know.

Perks.

.

.

Where is she again

A: She's at

She's at a special kind of work

B: Do you think I'm Mentally Fucking Challenged?

.

They make me vomit

.

Fish fingers.

.

They make me spew my guts up.

.

I don't eat fucking dead things. I don't touch things that were once living – even when they are called something sort of harmless and funny sounding like fish fucking fingers – though frankly eating something called fingers is heinous in itself – and I do not then cut them into bite sized pieces with a knife and a fork and I do not shovel them down my fat throat – How Did Your Throat Get Fucking Fat by the way – that is not a Natural part of the body to store So Much Lard on – I do not do all of that whilst the telly distracts me from the Outrageous barbarity of eating a creature.

.

A: What would you like to eat?

B: I'm not very hungry

Thank you.

A: .

You're upset

B: Nope

A: You have every right to be

B: That's sweet of you to give me permission to Feel whatever I am currently feeling

A: There are no rulebooks on how to do this 'B'

B: Bullshit. There are millions

A: Okay, well

B: I've got enough pamphlets on this shit to wipe your backside for the rest of your days would you like to borrow one

A: This is not my fault

B: Could you direct me towards the person who is to blame then please

A: Look, I'm not

B: Cos, as far as I can tell – She did something and She's locked up and I'm getting punished sat here with you eating murdered fish.

A: You're right, it's not fair.

It's rubbish.

I'm really sorry.

I'd like to help.

How can I help.

.

B: Piss off.

Just

Piss off.

Really, really quickly.

## 3. BAT.

**This scene is between five children (A, B, C, D and E).**

A: Instinctively

B: Shit

A: Instinctively

B: Shit

A: Instinctively, I'm going to say that this was a Bad idea

B: Shiiiiiiiit.

C: That was Insane

D: Are you alright

C: Jesus Christ

D: You're bleeding

B: That's just ketchup

D: No, she's bleeding

B: Isn't that just ketchup

C: No, she is definitely factually bleeding – that was Nuts

B: Shitting hell – she just

D: 'E'.

  Drop the bat

B: She just – You have Lost The Plot

A: 'B'

B: She Has – she has Properly Lost the plot

D: Can you shut up

B: But that was Properly Mad

A: 'B'

B: In a Good way – Mad in a Properly Good way though

D: Drop the bat

B: You are funny – 'E' 'E' 'E' – you are Proper Funny

D: Just drop the bat

A: What are you talking about Drop The Bat like you're

D: Just drop it

A: Like you think you're in The Wire

B: What's The Wire

A: DROP THE MIC

D: Shut up

C: DROP the bass bass bass bass

D: Jesus Christ

A: Drop Your Weapons

B: Your Trousers

D: 'E'. Drop it

C: She's bleeding

A: She's shaking

C: Are you crying

B: No, she's not crying, she's bloody brilliant, that was bloody brilliant – this is the Most Exhilarated I have ever felt

D: Seriously 'B', can you shut up

C: Most Exhilarated you've Ever Felt?

A: He's never had a wank

B: 100% not true 'A'.

C: That Was Mad

A: What were you thinking

C: She wasn't thinking, Evidently

A: Did you Seriously just ask what The Wire was?

B: I'm starving – did you get glass in the chips cos I'm properly starving

A: You're an idiot

B: Did it go in the deep fat fryer cos that'll be a royal pain in the ass

A: You are a Massive idiot

B: She's the idiot

D: Don't call her an idiot

B: Why? Cos she'll cave my head in?

D: No, cos she's not an idiot

B: She won't cave my head in

C: I'd have bet on her not having the balls to smash a shop up about half an hour ago but here we go

B: Ovaries

C: What

B: Don't say she's got balls – say she's got some serious Ovaries

I'm not joking. Bravery is not contained in a hairy ball sack.

A: They should put that on stationery.

D: Drop the bat

E: He just walked in.

.

He just walked in and asked for chips like he was anybody.

B: Who did?

D: Shut up

B: Who did though?

E: He came right up to the counter like he was a Normal person and he asked me to serve him Chips.

B: Do you Carry a bat round with you these days?

D: What part of shut the fuck up do you not get

B: She just smashed up a chippy and I'm supposed to not ask questions

C: She's traumatised

B: She's not traumatised

C: She's bleeding

B: She's talking about chip shop patrons like she didn't just smash up a shop – I'm bleeding

A: That's a paper cut

B: It really stings

E: He looked at me like he was normal and I was nobody

C: You're really bleeding – your wrists

E: I served him – I gave him fish and chips and I didn't ask him for money because how could I ask him for money after everything that's happened and he's standing in front of me like he's normal and I'm nobody

B: You sound deranged. She sounds deranged – I'm worried

D: Could you shut up quicker

B: I'm Concerned about her – I am expressing concern

D: Drop the bat

E: I meant to smash his head in.

        .

D: Alright.

E: I meant to smash his head in on his body. I meant for him to fold in half. I meant for his body to be here. Right here on the floor. Covered in his blood.

Not chips.

Not fucking glass and haddock and chips.

D: Alright. It's alright.

E: .

Is it?

        .

Can anyone else hear that.

Whistling.

There's a gap. There's a hole in my arm.

Can you hear that?

Is that just

Like Air.

Being Sucked through a pipe – can anyone else hear that?

It's burning. It's really burning.

Can you hear

Can you

Can

I.

## 4. TAPE.

**This scene is between two children (A and B).**

*A is holding a letter. Looks at it for a long time.*

*Opens it.*

*A cassette tape drops out.*

*Picks it up.*

*Looks at it.*

*A long time.*

*B enters.*

B: What's that?

A: Jesus

B: Not last time I checked – what's that?

A: .

Just fell out

B: What is it though? 'A'?

A: .

    Tape.

B: A tape

A: Yeah

B: A tape

A: Yes

B: And that Tape just Fell out

A: Yes

B: Fell out

A: Yeah

B: Just

    Fell

    Out

    .

A: Yeah

B: Of the fucking Sky, princess?

A: .

    Letter.

    It fell out of a letter

B: There we go

A: .

B: Got there in the end

A: .

B: A Letter

A: Yes

B: That Tape fell out of an Envelope containing a Letter now we're building a picture

A: Yes

B: A Letter

A: Yes

B: From your

A: Yeah

B: Your

A: Yeah

B: A letter from your Mum

A: Yeah

B: To you

A: Yeah

B: Ahhh.

A: .

B: Nice.

A: .

B: Ahhhhhhh.

A: .

B: That's nice, though, isn't it?

A: .

B: Quite Unusual, that is

A: .

B: Receiving Mail in here

A: .

B: Quite a Peculiar thing actually

A: .

B: So that's actually really really nice

A: .

B: You feeling a bit Conflicted about that

A: .

B: Bit all over the shop

A: .

B: Weird saying that

A: I don't

B: All over what shop, d'you know what I mean

A: I

B: You must be feeling funny about that

A: I

B: Feeling a bit funny

A: I

B: Yeah, you're feeling a bit funny about it

A: I guess.

B: Yeah, you guess. Yeah. You Guess.

Cos she's a proper headcase.

You must be feeling funny about it all on account of her being a complete fucking nutjob.

A: .

I just. Can I just. I just want to read it. Please.

Please.

B: Sure. Absolutely. Sure.

Jesus Christ.

You don't need my permission – are you asking for my Fucking Permission to read your own letter?

A: No. Just. A bit of space

B: To read your letter

A: Yes

B: How much space do you need?

To read your letter

What if I stand over here?

A: .

B: Or right back here?

A: .

B: Or I could face the wall – is that enough space

A: Head space

B: Sorry did you say Head Case

A: .

B: Does your Mother think it's 1992?

A: .

B: Is that why she's sent you a Mixed Tape?

A: .

B: How does she think you will be playing that?

A: I have a walkman

B: A WalkMan?

A: Yes.

B: And did she give that to you poppet?

A: .

Yes.

B: That's adorable.

That's Exceptionally sweet.

That's really nice.

That's great.

So you can hear her voice and that.

That's brilliant.

God.

That's properly heartbreaking that is.

.

So did she buy you that walkman before she stabbed that guy in the street for some smack, or After?

A: .

That's not what happened

B: Oh right

A: She didn't. She doesn't. She's not. Smack isn't. That's not.

B: You alright?

A: .

B: .

A: She's not on smack

B: You mean she's just Naturally that fucking crazy?

.

I could sort of understand stabbing some tramp in the fucking head because you're off your face on smack and Just Need Some More Of It – I can get my head around stabbing some tramp and putting your kid in a fucking Kids Home because you just find Smack so Deliciously Moreish, but just doing it for the Kicks.

Just doing it cos you just Fancy it?

.

That's Fucked Up.

.

A: .

B: I'm joking.

I'm just pissing around.

I'm just jealous.

Envious.

My Mum's dead.

Stone cold dead.

It's great yours is sending you stuff.

That's really nice.

That's just brilliant.

.

.

.

Can I have a look?

.

Sorry, did you not catch that – can I take a look?

.

Maybe there's a time delay – can I just have a look? I've not seen a letter in a long time. On account of my mother being deceased and all.

.

Perhaps all that smack your Mum was taking when she was pregnant with you has affected your hearing.

.

I'd just like to take a little look.

.

A: No.

B: Just a

A: No

B: Won't be a

A: No

B: If you just

A: No

> *B picks up the tape.*

> Can you

B: Just having a look

> *B starts to unspool the tape*

A: Please can you

> *B continues unspooling*

> Don't

> *B continues unspooling*

> Please

> *B drops the tape.*

> .

> .

## 5. T-SHIRTS.

**This scene is between four children (A, B, C and D).**

A: She's dead.

> .

B: Shut up

C: You're a dick

A: She's Blatantly dead

B: If you're not going to be

A: She clearly Died

B: Useful – if you can't be Useful then

C: You're making her upset

A: I'm sorry but she's definitely dead

B: Seriously, can you

A: I'm just being

C: A Penis

A: No – I'm just being

C: A Massive Penis

A: I just think she's dead

C: Yeah, you said that

B: About eleven times

C: You're really upsetting her

A: Why

C: Are you joking

A: No – I don't know why she's so upset about it

C: Because you keep saying the word Dead

A: Why're you so upset

B: Can you

A: No – come on 'D' – why're you so Upset

C: Could you be less of a Bellend 'A'

A: You didn't Know her – she didn't Know her

B: That's

A: No – but you didn't Know her – she didn't speak to you, you weren't Friends so

B: She's still allowed to be upset

C: It's a really shitty thing

A: Course it is – I'm not saying it's not

C: You're being incredibly casual about it

A: But – okay – it's. It's like you're a bit Excited

C: Shut up

A: Well it is

C: You're a Penis

A: It's like this is the most exciting thing to happen to you – this dead girl

B: Can you stop saying Dead

A: I'm being realistic

C: You're being a penis

A: Could you get a lot better at coming up with original insults really quickly

C: Penis is the most appropriate insult for you. I've landed on it really early and I'm sticking with it.

.

D: She's not dead.

.

A: I mean.

D: She's not

A: You're saying that like it's fact – do you Know something

D: .

   She's just not dead

C: She could definitely not be dead

B: Absolutely

A: I mean, I think she is definitely dead

B: We've established that

A: Alright

D: I don't think people who think she's dead or or Hurt or
   that we aren't definitely going to find her – I don't think
   those people should stay

A: Okay.

   .

   Okay.

   .

   I'll shut up.

D: I can still hear you thinking it

A: Alright. I'll stop thinking it immediately

D: Good

A: I've changed how I think about it entirely

D: Thank you

C: .

   .

D: I made T shirts.

B: Great.

They're great.

C: Brilliant.

B: Very clear.

A: .

Yeah. Really great. Well done.

D: Okay. Good. And signs – I've made signs

B: Right

D: And I've added to the Facebook page

C: Added

D: Yes, I've added some posts saying that we'll be out looking tonight – in the woods and on the marshes and down by the canal.

C: Right

B: Great

C: Good

B: Brilliant.

C: Well done

B: Yeah, well done

A: .

Absolutely excellent job.

.

D: She's done this before.

C: Yes

D: She has Form

B: Absolutely

D: So we should take heart from that – according to my
    research / she has

A: / Sorry

D: Be great if you could save your questions for the end 'A'

A: .

D: So, according to my research

A: Yeah – it's just you said research

D: She has gone missing Eight times before

.

   Eight times. I'll just let that

   Sink in.

A: Right

D: Yeah

A: Wow

D: Yeah

A: Research

D: So

A: You Carried Out Research

D: So

A: How exactly did you carry out research

D: So that puts us in an incredibly strong position

A: Strong position

D: That means we have an incredibly good chance of finding her

A: What're you

D: That means that She is is really likely to come home which is brilliant

A: What're you fucking Basing this on

D: Can you

A: No – what is this Actually About

B: 'A'

A: No – no – cos this is Weird – you didn't Know her.

I Knew her.

I sat next to her.

I walked home with her.

She fed our cat when we went to Lanzarote.

I Miss her.

You didn't even look at her.

You didn't even notice her.

You didn't even know she was fucking born.

And now she's dead.

Now she's definitely dead.

.

## 6. SINGING.

### This scene is for a child or two children or lots of children.

A child *(or lots of children)* sing *Under the Boardwalk* by the Drifters.

## 7. SEVEN.

### This scene is for one child.

*A child (A) is on the phone. Anxious.*

A: .

.

.

What took you so long?

Seven rings – that was Seven rings

Yes it was and that's not the – .

.

Are you okay?

Are you sure?

Are you outside?

Where?

In whose garden?

When are you going back?

What time?

Exactly?

Is that a person in the background? Who is it?

Are you talking to them? Have you talked to anyone?

Who?

When?

What about?

What did she say?

Then what?

And then what?

And what did you say?

And that was it?

Are you sure?

Have you got your keys?

Are you sure?

Can you check please?

Can you move them around so I can hear them?

Have you eaten?

Are you drinking?

Water?

Coke?

Not -?

Good.

Are you taking your medicine?

All of it?

Properly?

Have you got your coat on?

And a hat?

And you've got your keys?

Will you send a picture when you're back at home?

When will you get home?

Will you walk? Don't get the bus.

Don't wear headphones, you can't hear properly if you're wearing headphones and you need to hear properly when you cross roads.

Will you look both ways?

Every time?

And you'll be there when I get home?

Will you wait by the window so I can see you?

Will you?

Will you leave the curtain open?

Don't answer the door to anyone else, will you?

Have you paid the bills?

All of them?

Okay.

Okay.

Okay.

I'll call again in ten minutes. Put your phone on loud. And vibrate. Pick up quicker next time.

Okay.

Say I love you again.

And again.

And again.

And again.

And again.

And again.

Don't hang up yet.

Please don't hang up yet.

Please don't.

Please don't.

Please.

Mum.

## 8. PIZZA.

**This scene is between two children or one adult (A) and one child (B). 'A' should be older than 'B'.**

*A has been badly beaten up.*

A: I got pizzas.

The posh ones. The pepperoni where you can tell it's
Actually pepperoni.

And Rocket.

One of them has Rocket all over it.

.

I'll pick that off.

You always say that. Why do they put basically Lettuce on a pizza and expect it not to go rank when you cook it.

.

That's what you say.

What you always say. Rancid.

.

Dough balls.

Dips.

Crisps.

Ice cream. I got it all.

.

We can watch a film.

Or telly. We can watch something on the telly.

If you want to watch something on the telly?

Is there something you fancy watching on the telly?

B: Stop saying telly.

A: Okay.

B: It's weird.

A: Okay.

B: It sounds retarded

A: That's not a nice word

B: You sound retarded

A: I hate that word

B: You're a fucking retard.

.

A: Okay.

.

I might need your help.

Putting the pizzas in.

.

I might need you to help me out.

Putting the pizzas in the oven.

Cracked ribs.

B: Broken ribs.

A: Yes.

Broken ribs.

.

I am okay, you know.

.

I'll be alright.

B: .

A: It was frightening.

For you.

But I was okay – and I Am okay.

B: You're going to go back.

A: It's my job

B: It doesn't have to be

A: No.

But it does pay for posh pizzas.

B: That isn't even a little bit funny.

Or helpful.

A: No.

.

Hazard of the job

B: Getting beaten to shit?

A: I work with some Angry, Disenfranchised people

B: Jesus Christ

A: It's my Job to look after those people

B: No, you're supposed to put them in jail

A: I'd like to think it's more than that

B: You're Essentially supposed to lock up bad people

A: Sometimes I'm going to be on the receiving end of some
negative energy

B: He broke your ribs and stamped on your head

A: .

B: Negative Energy?

A: .

B: You're making it sound like he didn't want to do fucking
Downward Dogs with you in an Incense field or

A: That sounds like a fire hazard

B: The doctor said you're lucky you can still see, breathe and hear.

A: Pardon?

   .

   Jokes.

B: Stop it.

A: .

   He'll go to prison.

   For a really long time.

B: I'm not four.

A: I could tuck you in under my arm when you were four

B: No you couldn't

A: You were still Breastfed when you were four

B: Literally going to vomit in your face

A: That's fine. Just don't stamp on it.

B: You are so incredibly Unfunny.

   .

A: He had pinned his girlfriend up against the wall. When we got there, she had purple finger marks all across her neck. She was like, no no no, it's fine, they – the neighbour who called – made a mistake.

   Again.

   I've been there three times before.

Every time I see this woman she's been beaten up in some New way.

Body cam never picks anything up.

She's always Indignant.

He's always quiet. Polite. Let's her talk.

I don't want to press charges, there's nothing to say, yadda yadda.

I went there once and he'd pushed her face into her own vomit. She had vomit on her face.

He's kicked a baby out of her.

An actual fucking baby.

Out of her.

You shouldn't be able to Kick a baby out of a woman, that shouldn't be a physical possibility.

.

This time. She's hesitating. She's thinking about it. He's not completely thick, he's kicked her below the neck so we can't see it, but she is finding it hard to walk. She's on the edge of finally saying, yes please, yes please can you help me.

And he snaps.

.

Body cam.

Catches him kicking a door down, lifting me off the fucking ground and stamping on my head.

He'll go to prison now.

B: That's not how you're supposed to do your job.

A: No.

It's not.

B: You're an Awful police officer if that's how you think you get people put away.

'A'.

A: Agreed.

B: .

You're someone's Sister.

A: *(Smiles.)* Yes. 'B'.

I am Someone's Sister.

B: You're My Sister.

A: Yes.

Yours.

B: Give it up.

A: .

*Smiles.*

*Kisses B's head.*

No.

## 9. DOLL.

**This scene is between two children (A and B).**

*There is a pram with a baby in it.*

A: Okay.

B: Alright

A: Yeah

B: Definitely

A: Absolutely

B: Holy

A: YES

B: Shit

A: Yes again

B: That was epic

A: That was insane

B: You were brilliant

A: You Were

B: You just Took it

A: I know

B: Without even looking behind you

A: I know

B: You just Grabbed it and rolled it out of there

A: I know

B: She didn't even cry

A: I know

B: You're a natural

A: At kidnap or parenting

B: Fucking both mate.

A: Do you think it's a girl

B: Obviously

A: Right

B: Everything's pink

A: Yeah

   Yeah

   Yeah

   Could be hippies

B: Hippies

A: Sort of gender neutral

B: No.

   .

   Don't say kidnap again.

A: .

   Alright.

   .

B: She's sweet.

   Isn't she?

   She's sort of

   Sweet

A: I guess

B: You don't know anything about babies

A: And you do

B: Got a little brother

A: So you're an expert

B: More than you

A: Mary Fucking Poppins

B: Just saying she's sweet

A: Her face is a bit weird

B: She's just little is all

    Her face is just Little

    All babies have got faces like that

    Scrunched up and

    Sweet.

    Sort of

    Sweet.

    .

    She needs a name

A: She's got a name

B: Do you Know her existing name?

A: Obviously not

B: Alright then – she needs a new one.

A: Alright.

    NAME1.

B: Not a shit name, I didn't say – Come up with a shit name

A: Alright

NAME2?

NAME3?

.

NAME4?

B: You're mentally deficient when it comes to selecting names.

.

We'll call her Doll.

A: Doll?

As in

.

Doll?

I don't know about

B: That's her fucking name.

Doll.

A: .

B: Spell it.

A: .

B: Fucking spell it.

A: D – O – L – L.

B: Use it in a sentence.

A: .

The baby's name is Doll.

B: Perfect.

Doll.

.

Hello Doll.

## 10. WAITING.

**This scene is between two children (A and B),
or two adults.**

A: You alright?

B: Yep.

A: Not coming for breakfast

B: Nope.

.

Got a visit.

A: Oh

B: Yeah

A: That's great

B: Yeah

A: Your

B: Yep

A: All of them

B: No.

No.

But some of them

A: That's great

B: Yeah.

A: Great

B: Yeah

A: Yeah

B: Yeah.

Jesus, my mouth is dry.

A: Great

B: Thanks

A: That's really great

B: Thanks

A: D'you want me to get you anything

B: No, she'll bring stuff

A: Course

B: Or buy stuff, I mean

A: Course

Good luck with that

B: Thanks.

A: Can you bring me a Twix

B: Course. If she's got enough

A: Course

B: Course

A: Course. Thanks.

## 11. PARTY.

**This scene is between four children (A, B, C and D).**

A: You said Party

B: Yeah

C: You definitely said the word Party

A: We were expecting a party.

Like, a party Mid Party.

D'you know what I mean?

Not just you.

And a bowl of crisps.

That is a considerably sadder sight, than I was expecting.

D: .

I didn't say party.

A: 'B'?

B: Yes 'A'?

A: Did 'D' say party?

B: 'D' definitely said party.

A: I thought as much

C: I remember it very specifically because I was getting particularly bored of Mr NAME banging on about equations and then You said you had a free house

A: Thank you for that 'C' – that was remarkably clear

D: I didn't say Free house

C: You're Most welcome

D: I didn't Say Free House

B: You did

C: Fact

A: And Free House basically means party.

Doesn't it?

I mean, none of us think of anything else when someone says Free House

C: No

B: Not at all

A: Except shit loads of booze and a bit of Rihanna.

C: Not Rihanna

A: Shut up 'C'

C: Yes 'A'

A: Nothing wrong with Rihanna

B: Right

A: Rihanna has never made a Free House any worse

Is what I'm saying.

D: .

I didn't Invite you here

A: You left the door open

D: No I didn't

A: Alright, you left the door unlocked

D: No I didn't

A: Alright, you left a window open

D: No I didn't

A: Alright, you let me chuck a brick through it.

Which is pretty much the same thing as an invitation.

B: Correct.

A: And now you're being rude

B: Exactly

A: Now you're being really rude

C: I think so too

A: Which is a shame

B: Which is Weird

A: Exactly – thank you 'B'

B: You're welcome 'A'

A: It Is Weird to Invite people to your party and then not be a welcoming host

C: Not even a bowl of nuts

B: Not even some Taste the difference olives

C: My Mum'd be Mortified if she was in your position

B: Your Mum'd never be such a terrible host

Your Mum has always been a brilliant host

Your Mum hosted my dick really well in fact

C: Too far

B: I apologise

C: Thank you. I accept your apology.

A: See – now, maybe You could try apologising?

D: .

Apologising?

A: Am I not being clear?

B: You're being so clear

A: I thought I was being clear – We feel

B: Absolutely

A: That you owe us an apology for promising us a party. And then being this little sad case.

C: Agreed.

D: .

A: I mean. You should be flattered we even came.

B: Agreed.

A: You've got a long list of nicknames where – I'll be honest here – you don't come off that well.

.

C: Psycho

B: Yeah

C: Fleabag

A: You've had that since Primary School

C: Shitpants

A: That one is particularly unfortunate

B: Agreed

A: Did that one come about because you shat your pants? Is that right?

B: That is exactly the origin of that nickname – yes

C: Cumguzzler

B: That's really nasty

C: Mumfucker

A: Is that one because he has an amazing record for shagging hot Mums?

B: Nope. No, it isn't.

A: Oh that's right. It's based on the belief that you have shagged your Own mother

B: Yes exactly

C: Which is less cool

A: Don't get me wrong – your Mother's a very bangable woman

B: Absolutely

A: I mean, she's a real Piece

C: I agree

A: And from what I hear, Most people have had sex with your mother

C: Yes, I've heard that too

A: For a very reasonable price, I hear

B: Yes, I've also heard that information

C: Which makes it Fact, by the way

A: But You shouldn't be having sexual intercourse with her.
That's how horrible babies get made.

B: Quite.

C: That's presumably how you got made.

A: Very astute observation, 'C'.

C: Thank you, 'A'.

D: .

I'd like you to get out now.

A: .

Did you hear that?

B: I did hear that.

A: That's very upsetting.

C: That's very offensive.

A: That's literally last on the list of things to say to your
guests, just as they've got their foot in the door

B: That's very poor etiquette

C: Bad breeding

A: Of course. Mumfucker.

B: It all makes sense.

A: We work really hard

C: We do

A: We're Top Set for absolutely everything

B: We are

A: So we get pushed Incredibly hard

B: We do

C: That's an awful lot of pressure on a young person

B: It is

A: So we really need to let off steam in our down time

B: Agreed

A: I just finished my essay on globalisation for my Politics class

C: Congratulations

A: I'm likely to get an A

C: I don't doubt it

A: Because I get A's for everything

B: She does. You do.

A: So now I really want to find a way to relax

B: That's only fair

A: And I'd really, really like to do my relaxing with you

C: You should be very flattered

B: In your Free House

C: Exactly

B: At your Raging Party

A: It's a real rager

*B and C start to get bottles out of their bag. Line them up.*

I think we're going to have a really, really Brilliant time.

## 12. KISS.

**This scene is between two children (A and B) or two adults.**

*They stand opposite one another. Look at each other for a long time. They kiss.*

## 13. RED SAUCE.

**This scene is between three children (A, B and C).**

*Over the course of this scene they make dinner.*

*It can take some time.*

A: Can you chop that please?

B: Makes my eyes hurt

A: Put the goggles on

B: I look stupid

A: No one's looking at you

B: You are

A: We don't think you look stupid

C: Incorrect

A: 'C'.

B: How small

A: Red sauce small please

B: Okeydokes

A: Can you do the peppers

C: Where d'you get peppers from

A: Market – NAME gave me them

C: What size d'you want them chopping

A: Red sauce size

C: There are no knives

A: Use scissors – I put them on the side

C: Brill

A: How was school

C: Alright

A: Did you go

C: Course

A: What about you

B: Yep

A: Good.

Anyone ask about Mum

B: Nope

C: Nope

A: Good

B: Yup

A: Did you put your uniform in the washing basket

B: Yes

A: Good

   You?

C: Yep

A: What's tomorrow

C: Maths, Art, Reading, Swimming

A: Swim bag ready?

C: Course

A: Reading bag ready?

C: Yep

A: Any homework?

C: Did it.

A: Shall I check it?

C: If you like.

A: Can you pass me the sweetcorn please?

B: Where d'you get sweetcorn?

A: Corner shop. NAME2 gave it me. Said no bother.

B: That's my favourite.

A: That's what NAME2 said. Said, I know that 'C' likes it. So
   I said Ta and didn't look back.

   Gave me a box of Mini Milks too.

B: YES.

A: I know.

C: Result

A: I know

B: Smashing

A: I know

B: That'll get our calcium intake Right up

A: Oh right?

B: Science today

A: Good.

Great. That's really great.

.

Bit smaller please.

Can't take too much though. From people.

C: No.

B: Course.

C: No.

A: Don't want too many questions.

B: No.

C: Course.

B: No.

A: We're doing alright aren't we.

B: Yeah.

C: Course.

A: We're doing great really aren't we.

B: Yeah.

C: Bit quieter.

B: Yeah.

C: Quite like that though.

B: Yeah.

C: Getting a bit cold.

A: Come and stand near the cooker.

C: Can we put the heating on.

A: Not today. Save it till Sunday.

B: Can we have the telly on?

A: Not tonight. Jar's empty.

C: NAME3 says he can come round and fiddle the meter a bit.

B: That's good.

C: Good old NAME3.

A: Yeah.

B: Nice.

When will she be back?

D'you reckon?

Just so we know.

I don't mind or anything. We don't mind, do we? And it is nicer. We were saying that, earlier on.

And you. You're being. You tuck us in and help with homework and

Just.

Just be good to know if she's coming home.

A: .

I don't know 'B'.

## 14. FISHING.

**This scene is between two children (A and B).
A is fishing.**

A: I don't want to talk about it.

B: Fair enough.

That is Fair Enough mate.

.

That is Your Prerogative.

Prerogative.

Good word, that.

.

Must've been weird though

A: I don't want to talk about it

B: Must've been really sketchy though

A: .

B: Okay, kay, kay.

Got it.

Got

It.

Understood.

Fully

Understood.

Comprende.

Compos

Mentis.

.

Is that the [right word]

Yeah.

Yes.

On board.

.

.

So. Did they just, like, come up to you and grab you or

A: .

B: Cos everyone at school was

A: .

B: And I mean

It's pretty Epic

.

A: .

B: Yeah.

A: .

B: Did they read you your rights

A: .

B: Yeah.

.

Fair dos.

Fair enough.

Absolutely fair play.

Your call.

I Respect

Your call.

.

You ever actually catch anything

A: Yes

B: Nice

A: When it's quieter

B: Right

A: Right.

B: .

Do they have Ears?

Fish?

Can they Hear?

Is that what you

A: Probably help if you didn't throw stones

B: Right.

Sure.

Can do.

.

.

So I mean on this arrest thing

A: 'B'

B: Yeah – no but the thing is

A: 'B'

B: No, but

A: 'B'

B: See but

A: 'B'

B: Thing is – is that Everyone's talking about it

A: I don't want to

B: But Everyone is talking about it and Weird shit is getting
said so maybe it'd be good for you to put your story
out there.

I could set a few people straight

A: I don't want to talk about it.

B: Sure.

A: I don't know how to say that any clearer.

B: Sure.

.

.

Sure.

.

A: What kind of weird stuff

B: Thought you didn't want to talk about it

A: I don't

B: Right

A: Right

B: Good

A: Great

B: That's clear then.

.

NAME1 said she saw you going absolutely mental.

.

Apocalyptic.

.

And NAME2 said you were asking Mr NAME3 how to build a bomb in Physics.

Which.

If it's true is a fucking stupid thing to say. By the way.

And NAME4 said he saw you buying about five bags of nails in B&Q.

Which.

Again.

Unless you're dead into DIY, which, given the state of your house I'd say you categorically Aren't – is a really fucking stupid thing to do.

.

And then NAME5 – NAME5 said she Saw you kill a rabbit.

Literally, hands round neck, Kill a rabbit.

.

Which is

About as Nuts as it gets.

.

So. I reckon. If you Are doing all that stuff then maybe you should think about toning it down a notch.

.

Cos you look like a bit of a fucking nutjob.

D'you know what I mean?

D'you know what I mean though?

## 15. BLOOD.

**This scene is for one child or one adult (A).**

*A prison cell. A is pregnant. She is lying on a bed. She is in pain. She makes a noise, holding her belly.*

*She sits up. Cries out.*

*Shouts from other cells – Shut Up / You okay / What's going on / Shut the fuck up*

*She gets up, staggers to the door.*

*She begins banging on the walls, on the door.*

A: Hey. Hey hey hey – can

HELP.

Can. Help.

I

God

*She puts her hand between her legs. Blood. Lots of it. She starts to cry. Slides down the wall. Blood keeps coming. She puts her hand inside herself.*

Please. Please. Please. Please. Please. Please. Please.
Please. Please. Please. Please. Please. Please. Please.
Please. Please. Please. Please. Please. Please. Please.
Please. Please. Please. Please Please. Please. Please.
Please. Please. Please. Please. Please. Please. Please.
Please.

## 16. HOTEL.

**This scene is for two children or two adults or one adult (A) and one child (B).**

B: This is nuts.

A: .

B: This is Properly nuts – I've literally never been in a room This Fucking Fancypants before.

A: .

B: Stop grinning

A: You're happy

B: Your face though

A: That makes me happy

B: You look like the Cat That Got The Fucking Cream.

.

The bed's mega bouncy.

.

I'm not Saying anything about that – don't Look for Hidden Meaning there, I'm just saying that the bed is Really Bouncy.

.

Look at These Curtains.

That's insane. They've got like

Gold bits of of thread in them – is that like

Actual Gold?

.

No. Just thread.

Good though.

Good view. Isn't that a Good Fucking View? That's a real
– Breathe it in view.

.

*B exits into the bathroom.*

*Shrieks.*

'A'? 'A'?

*Comes back out again.*

Mini shampoo. Mini conditioner. Shower cap. Shower gel.
Moisturiser – fucking Posh Moisturiser And Exfoliator.

That's Nuts.

Have you Seen The Bath

*A shakes their head.*

It's Huge.

.

A: Big enough for two?

B: .

It's Massive.

A: Come here.

B: .

I've not had a bath in Years.

A: Come here.

B: We don't have a bath at home.

A: Come over here.

B: Just a shower.

And a shit one at that.

And there's always someone

Someone banging on the door every

.

every

.

every two minutes.

.

What?

.

You're looking at me all.

.

A: Come here.

B: This is really amazing.

I'm really grateful.

I'm really, really, really grateful.

I haven't said thank you yet and I wouldn't want you to think that I am ungrateful – I am really really thankful so.

.

Thank you.

A: .

You're welcome.

.

Come over here and say thank you properly.


B: .

    How did you pay for it.

A: With Money

B: Yeah but

A: With Cash

B: Yeah I

A: Did you see her face.

B: Whose

A: Girl on reception.

    Miserable fucking face.

    Til I threw the fucking Money at her.

    Then she perked Right up.

B: Yeah.

A: Silly cow.

B: .

    Yeah.

A: Silly cow

B: .

    Yeah.


A: Don't you think she was a silly cow

B: .

   Yes.

   .

   Yes I.

   .

   I mean.

   She seemed alright.

   Bit bored probably. But. alright.

   .

A: Right?

   .

   Bit weird of you to take her side

B: I'm

A: Bit weird of you to take some stranger's side when I'm
   paying for everything here

B: I didn't mean

A: Bit fucking Odd of you to side with that bint when I'm
   shelling out for a treat here and you barely remembered
   to say Thank You.

   .

B: She was a cow.

   .

   She was a Right cow.

A right grumpy, miserable, ratty, Shit excuse of a human being.

.

.

A: What d'you want to do.

B: .

Whatever You want to do

A: No.

You choose.

This is your treat.

My treat for You.

B: Um.

A: You've gone all shy.

.

B: We could go for a walk

A: .

A walk

B: We could go and look at the sea.

Pick shells.

Put our feet in the sand.

Could get fish and chips.

My treat.

I'll get them.

An ice cream.

Go on the rides.

Go dancing.

Look at the moon.

We could do anything.

Whatever.

Whatever we.

Whatever you want.

Really.

Whatever You want.

.

A: Pick shells?

B: .

A: You reckon I brought you here so we could Pick Shells?

B: I.

A: You reckon I Threw Money at that dickhead's face so we could build a sandcastle?

B: .

A: I'm teasing.

Your face.

I'm pissing around.

B: .

    I'm a bit tired.

    .

A: So?

B: .

A: What does that mean?

    I'm a Bit Tired.

    .

    You're not twelve.

    .

    I'm not twelve.

    It's only eight o'clock.

    .

    Just need some drinks in you.

    Then you'll be alright.

B: .

A: We could go get pissed.

    You're always more fun when you're pissed.

    Let's go get pissed.

    Sit on the sand.

    Then you can go and pick shells. Build sandcastles. Skim stones.

    And other retarded activities.

B: .

    I.

A: I'm Joking.

    I'm fucking Joking.

    Your face.

    Your little face.

## 17. BLOOD VESSEL.

**This scene is for two children (A and B).**

A: It was nice

B: Not really

A: It Was

B: It was hideous

A: I thought it was very moving

B: I burst a fucking blood vessel in my eye

A: Intense

B: When they lowered the

A: Very sad

B: Coffin and

A: Very moving

B: Everyone was throwing fucking flowers on it

A: Mine missed

B: And her Mother just Fell over

A: Her Dad was supposed to be holding her up

B: Well he wasn't doing a very good fucking job cos she just face planted the grass

A: Nearly followed the coffin six feet down

B: She Wanted to. She Wanted to go straight under. Be with her. She'd have dragged her up out of the coffin if she could've done

A: Maybe she should've shown as much motherly dedication when she was alive then

B: That is Dark

A: That is True.

.

Open Casket.

Brave choice.

Her neck was all blue.

You can cover a corpse in as many fucking bluebells and peonies as you like, you can't hide it's a corpse.

Particularly not if it's been left for bloody days by a river to rot

B: 'A'

A: Too far

B: Just a tad.

.

A: I thought it was a lovely tribute.

.

Lovelier than we might've guessed when she was alive

B: 'A'

A: S'true though.

.

She was So Sad.

So Profoundly Unloved.

Always said no one really noticed her.

Which was why she was such a Tremendous Nutjob – trying so bloody hard to get noticed.

And then here she is.

Dead and she's a real Hit.

Giant fucking funeral.

Flowers everywhere.

Weeping and Wailing and Hand Wringing and Singing – Jesus Christ the number of songs calling her an Angel.

Local news hiding behind every gravestone.

You – bursting blood vessels and lobbing flowers and telling her parents how much we Loved her.

I mean.

Don't you feel Awful for Lying so much?

B: Excuse me

A: Don't you feel like a massive Fraud for being such a fucking Liar

B: I wasn't lying

A: Don't you feel sort of Unclean and Disgusting for Lying through your Teeth

B: I burst a blood vessel

A: Oh I don't mean you weren't Crying, you were definitely
   Crying – I saw the tears Rolling down your face doesn't
   mean they were Honest tears doesn't mean the emotion
   you felt had anything to do with Her just means you
   are emotionally very suggestible and could never
   be a fucking spy or Doctor or anything because you
   Steal – emotionally – yeah – that's right actually, that
   Is what you – You Steal emotions because of your own
   anxieties or self esteem or or or – no actually – perhaps
   your awareness at how chronically underwhelming your
   life is – That is probably what you were Weeping at.


B: You're being Horrible

A: I hope she saw it.

   I hope she was looking down and finally felt some sense of
   achievement.


B: I hope she's peaceful.

   She liked singing.

A: Bullshit.

B: She used to sing

A: She also used to smoke crack – we didn't Know her.

B: I saw her singing.

   Drunk, off her face, swaying, out of her mind but Singing.
   And smiling. And I think she'd have liked the singing.

   I liked the singing.

I hope she liked the singing.

## 18. AWAKE.

**This scene is between two children (A and B).**

*B is asleep, face down in a plate of food.*

A: 'B'.

   'B'.

   'B'.

B: .

A: You fell asleep again.

B: Hm.

A: Need to try and keep your eyes open.

B: Yeah.

A: You've got baked beans literally all over your face.

B: mm.

A: It is almost funny.

B: .

A: .

   Hey.

   Hey.

   'B'.

B: I'm awake.

   I'm awake.

A: .

B: I'm awake.

.

So. How are you.

A: Don't.

B: Yep.

A: Don't even.

B: sorry.

A: Don't Pretend to be capable of holding a conversation.

B: sorry.

A: Just try and eat something.

B: Feel a bit

A: What

B: feel a bit

feel a bit

sick.

all the

all the time

.

A: You need to sit up.

B: Mmhm.

A: Have some water.

*B drinks.*

B: Sorry.

A: We have to do something about this.

B: N[o]

A: Wasn't a question

B: .

There's nothing [to do].

.

A: Hey. Stay awake.

B: .

sorry.

.

Nobody cares.

.

A: I care.

B: [That's] not enough.

A: I care enough

B: No. I mean.

Your caring. Isn't enough.

A: .

Is it stress?

B: Yes.

A: Are you ill?

B: Yes.

A: Is it the drink?

B: Yes.

A: And drugs?

B: Yes.

A: And them?

*B nods.*

A: They won't

*B shakes head.*

A: Leave you alone.

*B shakes head.*

A: You have to go to the police.

*B shakes head.*

A: You have to.

*B shakes head.*

A: Wasn't a question 'B'

B: Said they'd kill you.

.

Kill Mum.

.

If I went to the police.

A: We have to Try

B: No

A: I'll go

B: No

Threw a brick through Nan's window last time I said no.
Remember.

*B cries.*

A: I know.

*Smiles.*

I know.

It's alright.

I'm alright.

We'll be fine.


## 19. BISCUITS.

**This scene is between two children (A and B).**

A: Biscuits?

B: Yep.

A: Just biscuits?

B: Three packs of biscuits.

Three packs of Different Kinds of biscuits

A: .

B: Dodgers, Creams, Digestives.

The Holy Three.

You cannot tell me that is not a cracking selection.

A: .

    Yep.

    In terms of biscuits, you've really smashed it.

B: .

    What?

A: It's just not the most Practical thing.

    .

    You said you'd get sleeping bags.

B: Yeah.

    Yeah.

    My Dad's camping this weekend. Big bike trip. He took all the good ones.

A: Right.

    And the other stuff

B: Yeah

A: The Torch and the coats and the penknife and the

B: Yeah, he Swiped it all.

    Asshole.

A: Right.

    .

B: Sorry.

A: Right.

    And the uh.

The Money?

B: No, yeah, I looked in my Mum's purse but she just had a fiver and then I thought well that'd be a bit shit of me to steal her last fiver so I left it.

A: Right.

B: Yeah

A: Right.

.

Okay.

Okay. Okay.

B: .

You look a bit like you might

Cry.

Or

Have a Seizure or something.

A: .

B: We can still Do it.

We can still totally run away.

For a bit.

We'll just probably need to come back a bit quicker.

A: .

I don't want to come back.

B: Right.

A: I don't have anything to come back To, so

B: Right

A: So.

B: Yeah.

I mean.

I thought it was just going to be a bit of a laugh. So.

So.

Yeah.

.

Yeah.

## 20. SMASH.

**This scene is for one child or one adult (A).**

*A is stood in the middle of a room, holding a bat. They breathe in and out for a moment, nervous.*

*Then, they smash the room to pieces.*

## 21. TWEEZERS.

**This scene is between two children (A and B).**

A: She won't get out of bed.

B: Have you poked her

A: Yep

B: What with

A: Pencil.

B: Not good enough.

A: I have not finished telling you what I have been poking her with.

B: .

Please.

Continue.

A: .

I tried a pen

B: That is almost exactly the same as a pencil

A: Not finished you absolute Melon.

.

I hairdryered her arms.

B: Weird.

A: I tweezed some of the hairs on her big toe

B: Nice. Very nice

A: Didn't work.

She barely flinched.

Flicked her ankles

Twanged – yes I did say Twanged – I Twanged her forehead with an elastic band.

Nada.

.

So. Then I tried.

Lit match near her fingers

B: Jesus Christ 'A'

A: Then I freaked out that I was going to set the bed on fire

B: Legitimate fucking freak out

A: She shouted a bit then

B: What – she shouted when you set her On Fire?

A: She's not on fire

B: Currently?

A: I blew it out

B: Blew what out – her Body On Fire

A: No. The match. The match never

like

Ignited anything – I just put it a bit near her skin.

.

Threw some stuff at her head.

B: Like what?

A: A shoe.

A cabbage.

B: A cabbage?

A: Found one in the fridge.

Tried to throw the cat but it would not play ball.

Twat. The cat. The cat is the twat.

.

She's completely out of it.

.

B: How many bottles has she hidden?

A: One wine.

B: Not so bad.

A: Four cans.

B: Shit.

A: Some vodka.

B: Over how many days?

A: Dunno? Found it in the shower.

Found some empty cider cans In the bed.

Dirty cow.

She tells me off for leaving socks on the floor and then sleeps with cider cans In her bed.

.

Told me off.

She doesn't Tell me off for anything anymore.

.

B: .

Has she eaten?

A: Been sick

B: When

A: This morning

B: What was it?

A: From the look of it – toast and marmite.

B: Alright then.

That's a good sign.

.

What's she got today?

A: Meetings

B: Cancellable?

A: Already cancelled three of them.

B: Anything else?

A: House visits.

B: She can't do house visits.

A: Obviously not.

   Her notes said a toddler with a broken arm and burns on
   her scalp.

B: That's horrid.

A: Third hospital visit in two months

B: That's fucking horrid

A: Her job Is horrid.

   That's the whole point.

B: Email her boss

A: She's getting pissed off

B: Obviously she's getting pissed off but we don't have much
   choice.

A: I'm not doing it.

   It's your turn.

   Your shift is literally starting now.

I need to sleep.

B: I know you do.

A: I've been watching her to make sure she doesn't choke on her vomit – I need to sleep now

B: I'm sorry.

A: .

It's alright.

.

How'd your exam go?

B: Fine. I think.

I'll be a fully qualified lawyer in about seven years and then we'll be saved.

A: You'll be out of here.

That's the main thing.

You'll be long gone.

And I'll be long gone.

You'll be defending murderers for shit loads of dollar and I'll be working checkouts and we'll live in a big house with a yellow door and I'll do all the cooking and you'll do all the cleaning.

Or.

You'll pay for all the cleaning.

And.

She can die in her own vomit and we'll be far away.

.

I don't mean that.

B: I know you don't.

A: Except sometimes I do mean that.

B: I know.

A: I really, really, really, really, really, really, really, really
love her.

.

I just also fucking hate her.

.

B: 'A'.

.

She's going to get sacked.

And then she'll be miserable.

And she'll drink More.

Except there'll be no sorry's or Attempts to get better.

And there'll be no money.

And we'll be fucked.

.

We have to get her Up.

.

.

A: I'll try the tweezing again.

## 22. DANCE 1.

**This scene is for children.**

*A group of children dance to something like Fuck The Pain Away by Peaches. Or similar. Their dancing doesn't have to match the song. It might be quite balletic.*

## 23. PINK LEMONADE.

**This scene is between two children (A and B).**

A: Where's your Mum.

I won't tell.

I promise.

I'm not a total dick you know, you can Trust me.

B: Do you want a lemonade

A: No.

B: It's pink.

A: Makes shit all difference, I'm not seven.

So.

Where is she?

Why're you living with your weird Aunt?

B: She's not weird

A: She was doing the loudest dump in your toilet earlier on. It's like she's never lived with Actual people before.

B: She hasn't. Not really. She's alright. Everyone shits.

A: I don't.

B: Oh right.

A: You're literally so disgusting talking about faeces.

B: You definitely started it.

A: I'll tell you a secret.

    If you tell me where she is.

B: Why d'you care so much

A: Cos I'm your friend and I'm worried about you living here
   with your bowel incontinent Aunt

B: You're obsessed with her arsehole

A: I'm not

B: You sound like you're doing a phD in Anal Studies

A: You do know that that's something else really specific don't
   you?

B: .

A: I mean, I know you think that that sounded really funny
   but actually you're making a pretty offensive accusation
   there about my sexual preferences and it's not cool.

B: .

    Still sounded quite funny.

A: It didn't.

B: .

    I mean. It did.

A: She's in prison.

  You Mum is in prison.

  My mum already told me.

  Literally everyone knows.


B: Then why're you Asking me

A: Cos I wanted to see if you'd tell.

  And my secret was that NAME1 fingered me at a party on
  Saturday and it was literally the most heinous experience
  of my life. He jabbed upwards like he was directing traffic
  Northbound on the M6. So. I trust you.

B: I already knew about that.

  You talk about yourself All the time – you told me that
  yesterday.

A: Still. Proves I trust you.

B: It's not the same thing – those stories are not the same
  thing.

A: What did she do?

B: Why the M6? You said M6 yesterday as well, what about
  his technique made you think of the M6?

A: Don't know. Sounds right, doesn't it.



  What did she do

B: I don't know

A: Bullshit

B: I don't want to know

A: If I literally just type her name into Google it'll tell me what she did

B: Which means you already know

A: It's pretty dark.

   How long's she got?

B: Stop asking me things you clearly already know the answer to.

A: .

   Five years is ages.

B: Do you want a lemonade?

A: If she's good then she'll get out quicker though?

   Isn't she having a Baby?

   Won't they let her out when she has the baby if she's good?

   Are you going to go and see her?

   Have you seen her already?

   .

   Did you see it happen?

   .

   It says all over the Internet that you were there when it happened.

That when he crawled out the door and blood was everywhere, you were still sitting on the floor.

In Shock.

They often say 'In Shock' like they were there with you and could see that you were In Shock.

.

I'm just trying to be your friend

B: Then stop asking me about it.

A: .

I won't tell anyone.

B: You said literally everyone knew already.

A: Well. I'll stand up for you then.

B: Great.

Thanks.

I appreciate that a lot.

A: Even though you don't want to tell me anything.

B: Nope.

A: Were you there then?

Like they said?

When she

B: I am going to have a pink lemonade.

A: .

Have you got any gin?

## 24. OKAY.

**This scene is for children (A and B).**

A: I'm not here

B: Right

A: I really shouldn't Be here

B: Okay

A: My parents would absolutely fucking End me

B: Sounds intense.

A: .

    I wanted to see if you were okay.

B: .

A: You seem a lot not okay.

    You seem like the total opposite of okay.

B: .

A: And. I know we don't speak much.

    Or at all.

    But. I just thought you might Like to know – it might Help you to know that someone had noticed that you seemed

    Not okay.

    .

B: Okay.

A: .

    Someone said something about you making a bomb.

Someone said something about you and a Rabbit.

.

Someone said something about you and your Mum not being around and.

.

I just wanted you to know that I was here.

Here.

Now.

And Here in a general sort of a way.

.

If that was.

If that was.

Any.

Use or Comfort or.

.

To you.

.

## 25. DEAD.

This scene is between three children (A, B and C).

*C is crying.*

A: .

.

Oh shit

B: what

A: it's Just hit me

B: what has

A: The meaning of life.

B: .

A: Did that happen to you too?

B: .

    No?

    I don't think [so]?

    no?

    no.

    that didn't happen.

    my chest really hurts but.

    .

A: It just Landed on me with Absolute Clarity

B: right

    gosh.

A: It Came Over me in, like, this Wave of knowledge

B: yes

A: in the way that people Talk about, you know, like a a a

    Religious experience?

B: mmm

A: And I just

Obviously

wasn't Expecting it

B: no, obviously

A: I was sort of Preoccupied

B: yes

A: with what had just

B: yes

A: though.

.

Weirdly.

.

I'm sort of Struggling to Remember what just.

.

That feels very sort of.

.

No Edges.

.

In fact.

.

I've got Absolutely no idea what just happened – I Know
Something happened, something Momentous happened,
but actually I don't know What happened.

.

I've been completely thrown by the fact I've landed on what the meaning of life is.

.

B: sure.

that makes sense.

A: .

why is she crying?

B: .

I think because it still hurts maybe?

A: .

right.

B: .

are you not in pain?

A: .

I don't think so?

.

B: try and breathe in.

A: *Tries.*

*Can't.*

.

oh.

that's odd.

B: *nods.*

A: I feel sort of.

.

water.

just water.

B: *nods.*

that's what you Look like too.

A: *nods.*

.

oh.

are we.

B: *nods.*

I think so.

yeah.

.

A: is it permanent, do you think?

B: *nods.*

*shrugs.*

I mean.

no way of knowing for sure.

but.

it always Sounded pretty permanent, didn't it?

A: *nods.*

that's a shame.

B: *nods.*

   *shrugs.*

   it was pretty miserable. Most of the time.

A: *nods.*

   No, just.

   Like, just when I've discovered the Meaning of life, that's when we die.

   that's a shame.

B: that Is a shame.

A: I sort of would have wanted to Tell people what it was.

B: yes.

   that's fair enough.

   .

   you could tell us.

A: .

   I've forgotten.

B: .

   oh.

A: .

   just.

   when I remembered what Happened.

   with the water.

   and the Knife.

and the Pushing.

.

then I forgot all about the Meaning.

B: yes.

that makes sense.

A: .

but it Was a nice feeling. Knowing it.

B: yes.

A: I think it was a Good reason. We're on Earth for a Good reason.

B: right.

A: which is.

Good to know, isn't it?

B: yes.

I guess so.

A: when - you're right - so much of it feels so awful so much of the time.

B: .

yes.

A: will it stop bleeding do you think?

B: .

I don't know.

## 26. PREGNANT.

**This scene is for two children or two adults or
one child (A) and one adult (B).**

A: Could you just not look at me for a minute

B: .

A: Could you just turn and face the wall or or look at your
shoes or close your eyes or put your hands over your
eyes – just for a minute – cos I want to say something and
I'd really much rather you were not looking at me or even
in my general direction actually – whilst I say it.

B: .

A: And. I'm going to say something now – I'm going to say
The Thing now and again – I'd really appreciate it if you
just Did Not have a reaction – or at least a reaction that
is visible or audible. Obviously, I imagine that you will
experience a reaction and I'd just like you to contain that
response in a very internal way for the time being because
what I have to say is fairly big information that I am still
figuring out my response to and I really do not have the
space – emotionally or mentally or otherwise – to deal
with Your responses.

B: .

A: I can feel you having responses. Which. Given I have Just
made the request I can sort of understand as I assume you
are Processing, so I'm just going to give you a moment to
Gather yourself and stop having such Obvious Opinions
on what I am saying.

B: .

A: .

I am pregnant.

I am Having a baby. Which means I'm keeping the baby.
Just so we're very clear – I used those words – Having
A Baby so that you wouldn't be under any Illusion that
I would be Not Having it.

Cos I'm having it.

The alternative has never entered my head.

Maybe.

It's been a shock. Clearly. Obviously, I was Profoundly
Fucking Shocked to discover I was pregnant. Sorry for
swearing. And, Initially, perhaps, perhaps Immediately
after the discovery I did think about Not having it maybe
maybe I thought about that a tiny tiny amount just for a
split fucking second – sorry – of a moment and what that
might mean and what life might be if That was the route
taken and I'll be honest it felt Bigger and Full of Possibility
and a Bit like taking a Big Breath of air in a tulip field or
something lovely like you'd find on the front of a card
or something – as opposed to the choice of Having it –
which, I'll be honest – feels a bit like just deciding all of a
sudden to say No to everything that I might have sort of
imagined for myself in a really small way, Having it, the
choice to Have it feels perhaps like life like like Life will
be a series of narrow airless corridors one foot in front of
the other, heel to toe, for the rest of my days – but I think
that's also just about me Repositioning my expectations,
I think that Feeling, that sudden lung flattening ankles
bound mouth taped up Claustrophobia I am feeling is
about me having to Redirect the hopes and aspirations for
my life – and hopes and aspirations like having a regular
fucking income – sorry – or being able to go on holiday
or or or amounting to More than people have expected
me to – I had been relying upon those hopes and those

aspirations as though they were solid, tangible, immovable markers in my future – places I was Looking Forward to Getting to – whereas actually they were just thoughts and thoughts are not solids or walls and this baby will need Solids and Walls and maybe I had pictured – and no, sorry, I can Feel you fucking responding again – so maybe just turn around, face the wall and look at your feet – Sorry Baby For Swearing – Maybe I had Pictured being a Mother in a very different kind of way – Maybe, Honestly, Maybe I had a sort of Earth Mother image going on – flowers and long hair and a house with central heating and a bedroom that could become a beautiful nursery with mint green curtains and lemon yellow walls and rocking chairs and you know – things that cost money – and actually that's not a Realistic Vision of Motherhood and not a vision of Motherhood anyone I actually know in real life has any kind of tangible experience of and and so I think I would have had to make my peace with that at some point anyway so that's not really reason I suppose reason to not have it would have something to do with how Shit I feel or how Profoundly Lonely I feel or how Unequipped I feel or yes or mostly how completely Lonely I feel. I think. Yeah. Yeah.

Yeah.

Is that normal?

.

Is that. Is that how it's supposed to be?

.

.

Cos that's.

I.

So that's.

Yeah.

## 27. CARRIER BAGS.

**This scene is between two children (A and B).**

A: This is my stuff.

B: Alright.

A: The stuff over here

B: Alright

A: On This side of the room – this is mine

B: Okay

A: In these carrier bags

B: Alright then

A: You're not to touch them

B: I wasn't planning on it

A: I'll know if you've touched them

B: Then you'll know that I haven't

A: I'll know immediately

B: I have zero interest in touching your carrier bags

A: There are seven of them – okay

B: Yep

A: Seven. Got that?

B: Seven.

A: Fast learner.

B: .

Was that a joke?

A: I don't joke about my stuff.

I don't generally joke.

That may be useful information for you to have about me.

B: I'm delighted to receive it.

A: They're all the same colour, so it's really easy to remember. Don't touch the blue carrier bags.

B: I couldn't give a crap about your carrier bags

A: They contain all my worldly possessions

B: Well that's just the saddest thing I've ever heard

A: You must not be familiar with famine and war and the current situation in Syria in that case.

B: Not as sad as your carrier bag situation.

A: And maybe we should put some kind of markers down the middle of the room in order to indicate what is yours and what is mine

B: Fine

A: I don't know if you have any suggestions about what we might use as a marker in order to make that division clear.

B: No.

A: .

I mean. Tape is the obvious answer – Obviously

B: Knock yourself out.

A: Okay.

So. I'll provide the tape on this occasion – I have
Coloured tape as that was the system with the last guy
too – but if it needs replacing, I would ask you to finance
that one.

B: Great.

A: Good.

And I'll stop the marked section just before the door, so
it's clear that we can Both use the door

B: That's a swell idea

A: Just so there's no confusion

B: That's very clear

A: And, I'd suggest we both think of the division more in
terms of Stuff.

I don't mind – for example – if your foot crosses the line
into my section of the room every so often

B: That's very good of you

A: I think being Militant about that would be silly

B: Agreed

A: But your Stuff – your Stuff must not come into my bit of
the room, and my stuff must never be in your bit.

Okay?

B: Fine.

A: Great.

B: Good

A: Great.

Are you scared?

B: Of what?

A: Most people are a bit scared. I think. That's what my last foster Mum said, she said mostly new things and new situations make people scared and that that might be what's really going on if they end up being a bit short with you or or unfriendly or

B: No. I'm not scared.

.

A: Good then

B: Good

A: Good

Good.

.

I'm 'A'.

B: Good for you.

## 28. QUEUE.

**This scene is for two children (A and B).**

A: Hundred and thirty three seconds.

.

That's how long we've got. Give or take.

.

Maybe less. She's pushing in. She's trying to push in. I can see her pushing in.

Jesus.

Why would she be pushing in? Also – why would She
be pushing in Here – she has been Losing Her Shit all
week – panicking about getting beat up on the bus here
or or getting Robbed – she made me take my watch off
and wear my shittest trainers. She was Trying to get me
to wear a Bumbag for God's sake – I don't know what
she thinks BumBag is like Prison Code for but now look
at her, all sense has gone out the window and she is
Pushing in – she is Pushing a Granny out of the way in a
queue for a Vending Machine in a Prison as though she
is not a person who Loves queuing so why is she now
breaking the rules so flag rantly – it suggests an entire
disregard – no, Contempt – for the system – which I
Know is not the case – there is a woman, there is our Dear
Mother who Believes in, Respects – Lives by the Queuing
system – feels Outraged when she spots or or – even
worse – Senses another person Priming themselves for a
push in – and yet, There she is. Shoving that Old Lady.

All that

Violence for the hope of a pack of Revels.

Probably not Revels.

Revels aren' t really a Vending machine regular. Are they?
Maybe. Maybe they are.

.

I'd say we were left with around ninety seconds.

.

And. And that number is just going to continue to

Plummet so.

.

That is what time Does. That is what happens to time. It just. Drops off. Drops off the face of.

'NAME1' got a rabbit. White one. Black ears. It's pretty fat. Seems like a bit of a dickhead to be honest – bit 'NAME2's finger and didn't seem remotely apologetic about the whole affair.

'NAME3' dumped 'E'.

.

And

B: Please stop talking.

A: Absolutely yes.

Sorry.

.

B: Have you ever felt like you were standing exactly to the left of your life?

Like.

Your life is there. Just there.

.

And you're Here. One foot Almost in it, but Not.

It's. It's like you are So Palpably Not in your life, even though you have Proximity to it – you Are next to it you Are shoulder to shoulder cheek to cheek with it, you can

Almost

Feel it.

You Can Almost

Feel your life.

You Can Almost Feel Your Life – Its Breath. Almost.
There. By your Ear. In. And Out.

And so it must Be there, you must be occupying it –
occupying your life I mean – because that is how it works
isn't it that Is how Life Happens isn't it.

Isn't it?

Is it?

.

A: I don't.

I don't know.

I'm not sure I

B: I feel like that All the time

A: Okay

B: Constantly.

A: Okay.

.

And you

Don't want to feel like that

B: That's not the point

A: It's not the point.

B: It's just a fact

A: Right

B: It's just the most factual thing I can describe to you right
now

A: Okay

B: I'm not Qualifying it or

A: Okay

B: You don't understand

A: I'll be honest, I don't.

    But I'd like to – I'd like to understand and you'd like me to understand

B: I have asked them to remove my TV.

A: .

    Okay.

    Is that. Is that Related to

B: I have asked them to take it away Three times.

A: .

    Okay.

B: I don't think they can See me.

A: .

    'B'. Pretty sure they can See you

B: Or Hear me

A: I can Hear you – 'B' – I can Hear you and

B: They can't. Or they are choosing not to

A: Can you. Look – Mum'll be here in a

B: I spoke to the Chaplain

A: .

That's. Alright. I won't call that Mental but that does
Sound a

B: I spoke to the Chaplain and I asked Him to take the Telly
away

A: I don't think

B: I know exactly how to electrocute myself using a television.

A: .

Please can you not say that.

B: It would be very very very Easy for me to do that to
myself.

A: I'm not. I'm.

B: That would genuinely be a very straightforward activity

A: Activity is a fucking stupid word for

B: I could Achieve that and then this would be done with and
I, look, I just – I Dwell on that. A great deal.

A: .

B: They don't check on me as regularly as they ought to.

A: I will. We will Talk to them about that 'B' – that is
something that Mum and me can talk to them about

B: They can probably See and Hear you

A: They can See and Hear you

B: They took away my bedding

A: Okay

B: They didn't want me to Hang myself

A: Okay, look

B: But then they've left the telly in there

A: I'm finding this – Okay

B: Which feels a bit like removing the bomb

A: Don't say bomb

B: But Handing over the loaded gun – do you see

A: This is.

   Look.

   You're not well.

B: I agree.

A: You won't feel like this forever.

B: I agree.

A: I can. We can Help – we can Do things to help you

B: Take my telly away.

A: I promise I will do Everything I can to to. To Do that.

B: .

   Once the telly is gone then they need to get rid of the stairs.

A: .

   The stairs

B: And the glass

A: What glass

B: And the razors

A: There shouldn't be any fucking razors In here what're you

B: And this table leg

A: I

B: Chair leg

A: Okay

B: And my brain. And my heart. I need someone to
restructure my heart and rewire my brain so that
Everything – and I mean Everything – doesn't look
like a way to get out – because right Now, this minute –
Everything, every Single object just seems to be uncurling
itself, unfolding itself and revealing its potential to do me
harm. To lead me out – not gently – not painlessly – not
Kindly or Simply – I do Understand that if I were to press
this table leg through my throat or my skull or my heart
it Would Hurt and I Would Bleed and it would be Slow
but it would be Out. Eventually. It would be a Way Out.
It would be an End. It would be a Climbing out of what is
nearly, barely a life and it would be a Finish. A Finish.

.

A: It will be okay. It might all be okay.

B: *Smiles.*

*Nods.*

## 29. PROM.

### This scene is for two children (A and B).

A: Stop laughing

B: Not laughing

A: You're literally pissing yourself laughing

119

B: Zero piss on me mate

A: Metaphor

B: Don't say literally then

A: Stop Laughing

B: Not laughing.

   Definitely

   Not

   Laughing.

   But that was stupid funny.

A: It wasn't, it was Annoying

B: Sure sure – I mean – what did she say – you can't leave
   your room for about a Year

A: Two months

B: Social Suicide

A: It's not that big a deal

B: I mean. She thinks it is. And Two Months covers all the
   end of exams stuff

A: Got that

B: Prom

A: Yeah got that too

B: I mean

   Fucking Prom

A: Noted

B: Who doesn't go to their Own Prom

A: The coolest people

B: Bullshit

A: Maybe she'll change her mind

B: She had to Come And Pick You Up At A Police Station 'A', I have Literally Never seen her so angry and I am not using the word Literally incorrectly by the way – she was Purple and her Moustache was Quivering – like Properly Quivering

You are Not going to Prom.

.

NAME1 might dump you, mightn't he?

Yeah. Probably. If you can't see him for a month and you can't even go to Prom, NAME1'll probs dump you won't he.

A: Give a shit. I'll just get another one.

B: Bold.

That's pretty bold.

It took you long enough to get NAME1'll to go out with you and he is absolutely gross so I don't think you'll be able to just 'get another one'.

.

I mean.

.

It's a bit sad though, isn't it. I mean. You got cuffed coming out of Superdrug. I Literally – and again, I do not misuse the word – I Literally cannot think of anything more humiliating than getting Arrested in a Superdrug for stealing some tweezers.

A: Alright

B: Your brows aren't that bad babe, they could use a tidy for sure, but they don't seem so dire that you would need to emergency rob some tweezers to deal with them then and there.

Or was it for the thrill? Did you nick the tweezers purely for the buzz?

A: Stop laughing

B: I mean.

I mean.

I would try to.

But it is Literally the funniest thing that's happened all year. So. Yeah.

## 30. WAITING AGAIN.

**This scene is for two children or two adults.**

A: You not gone yet

B: No.

A: They not called you

B: Not yet.

A: Oh.

Want me to

B: No.

Thanks.

## 31. NOTHING.

### This scene is between two children (A and B).

A: What did you say

B: I don't know if I'm allowed to say

A: Course you're allowed to say – what did you say

B: Same as what you said

A: How do you know

B: Cos you said.

Cos she said.

I just what she said to say – what You said to say.

A: .

B: That Nothing happened.

A: .

B: That it was an accident.

A: .

B: That I'm very clumsy.

A: .

B: That I just walk into stuff and fall over a lot.

I think I was really convincing – I think they're going to run some tests.

Someone said something about Motor Neurone Disease.

A: Are you Kidding me

B: Think I laid it on a bit thick.

I was very convincing.

.

Don't cry.

A: Your leg's fucking broken

B: Yes

A: She can't come and see you cos her face is purple

B: That's alright. I've got you.

A: I don't want you to have me – I don't want to be your
person

B: .

Alright.

A: I Will Be.

Obviously.

But I shouldn't Have to be. Shouldn't have to be your
One person.

She should be.

It should be Her.

She's your Mum, she's my Mum.

In that she Birthed us.

Not that she's doing anything particularly Maternal these
days.

Like protecting you.

Like stopping him throwing you down the fucking stairs.

.

You should have told them the truth.

B: You said not to

A: I know

B: You categorically said Not to tell them the truth that's why
I said a load of stuff that I had made up about falling over

A: Yes because I don't know what's worse.

Because I haven't figured out what's worse.

Home.

Or not home.

.

B: I don't understand.

A: .

You shouldn't be fucking here.

Neither should I.

## 32. BLUE.

**This scene is between two children (A andB).**

A: Is that an arm?

B: .

A: Shit.

B: .

A: Oh my God.

Shit.

Is that.

Shit.

Can you.

'B'.

Shit.

That's an.

'B'.

'B'.

That's an arm. That's an Actual Arm – that's a.

B: Don't touch her

A: She might need help

B: Don't touch it though

A: What're you talking -

That's a Human Arm it's

It's blue

B: Exactly, it's blue – it's clearly a dead arm

A: You still have to

B: Still have to what

A: I don't know I

B: Shake it?

A: No I. Help it

B: I don't think we're supposed to touch it

A: Help somehow – we still have to – what d'you mean
   Supposed to

B: I mean we're not supposed to

A: I don't think there's a Supposed to in this situation

B: Of course there's a Supposed to – it's a it's a a a Crime
Scene, isn't it

A: Crime Scene

B: Yes a fucking crime scene

A: We should check for a pulse

B: It's blue

A: I know it's blue, you've said it's blue, I'm still checking for
a pulse.

.

Jesus.

Oh my.

She's dead

B: Obviously

A: She's dead

B: Obviously she's dead

A: She's covered in leaves

B: I can see that

A: She's completely covered in leaves

B: Can you see her face

A: .

No.

Yes.

A bit.

Jesus.

Yes.

Her eyes are open

Fuck

I'm going to be sick

B: Get away from it then

A: Her

B: If you're going to be sick get away from it

A: Her – it's a Her

B: We should call the police

.

That's what you're Supposed to do, you're supposed to call the police.

A: I haven't got a phone.

Mum confiscated it.

Bitch.

B: Can you focus a

A: Sorry

I'm a bit in shock

B: I haven't got any signal

A: I'm a bit in shock I think

B: I can't get signal

A: I shouldn't have said that

My Mum. She's not a.

Sorry.

Her ankles are blue

She's really really dead

She looked wet

B: Jesus

A: She looks cold

B: She's dead – she's not feeling the cold

A: Anymore

B: Anymore – exactly.

A: I want to put my coat on her

B: That's mental. That is a mental thing to do

A: I said Want to – I said I want to

B: She's dead

A: I know she's dead, I touched her arm, I know she's dead.

.

Maybe we should say something

B: Like what

A: I don't know. A prayer. Or a poem or something.

B: You've fully lost it

A: She's dead – I am trying to imagine being dead and wondering what I might like

B: Are you on glue

A: I would want someone to hold my hand

B: She doesn't Want anything she's Dead

*A kneels down.*

Maybe we should just go

A: To stroke my hair.

To say something.

With kindness.

To say it will be okay.

I think that I would find that peaceful. If I were dead.

.

*A Sings.*

## 33. LEISURE CENTRE.

**This scene is between four children (A, B, C and D).**

A: So he looked at my tits.

B: Who

A: 'NAME1'. Obviously.

C: Obviously

D: Obviously.

B: Right

C: Nice

D: Intense.

B: .

On purpose?

A: Yes on purpose, how would that happen by accident?

B: .

My brother once caught a look by accident.

We were playing sharks in the swimming pool. You know.
Where one of you goes right to the bottom and swims
underneath the other one for ages and then. I dunno
actually – the game itself doesn't have clear rules or
anything but

C: 'B'

B: Right – anyway. My bikini fell down. Should Have Seen
His Face.

He was So Confused. Cos they're just Tits, right, and he
Loves tits. But then there's my head about half a metre
away from them and he could not handle that. Didn't
speak to me for about a month.

A: You reckon me and NAME1 were hanging out in our
swimming costumes and he just Happened to see my tits?

B: No.

I dunno.

Were you at a Leisure Centre when this happened

A: No. Obviously not – Obviously we're not hanging out at
leisure centres

B: I don't know do I

C: The leisure centre is shit

D: True

C: And not where you go if you want to Do sex

D: Do sex

C: Yeah.

A: Do Sex?

C: Or nearly sex or or looking at tits which is sort of on the way to sex isn't it?

.

D: Hang on, you think your head is Half A Metre away from your tits

B: .

Thereabouts.

Give or take.

D: You're so spectacularly thick. It's like having a pug. I might put a lead on you.

B: I'm not very good at geography.

D: Geography?

C: Where did it happen if not the leisure centre?

B: I Just said I'm not good at geography

C: Obviously I'm not asking you unless you were present for the tit viewing, I am asking 'A'.

A: .

His flat.

C: Oh

D: NAME1's flat?

A: Yeah

D: Your boyfriend has a flat

A: Yep

D: That is very cool

A: Yes

D: Your brother's a perv by the way

B: I know. Major.

D: Your boyfriend has a Flat man

C: See – flat's are sexy. Leisure centres are not

D: Shut up

C: Right.


B: They Are massive

A: Sorry?

C: The flat is massive?

B: Tits – your tits Are massive

A: .

   Thank you?

B: I just mean Most people have Looked haven't they, they're
   proper sort of sock tuckers

A: Excuse me

D: Sock tuckers?!

B: It's a compliment – it's a – I just mean. Loads of people
   have seen your tits

D: I mean, we get that You've looked at them, you're making that weirdly clear

B: My point is, that it's Hard not to

D: I manage to look at her face, I just Raise my head about half a metre up

B: Shut up – I just mean – the fact her Old boyfriend has had a look isn't exactly news

D: 'B'

A: I'm Right Here guys

C: Did you mind?

A: .

Mind what?

C: Him looking?

B: Doubt it

A: Shut up.

.

No.

Not really.

.

I was pretty fucked

B: You're always pretty fucked

A: .

B: Didn't mean that in a Bad way – you're loads more fun now

A: .

B: You've always been Fine but now you're like Fun.

D: 'B'

B: What

D: You're being a Tit

B: Jeez. I'm being Nice. I'm paying Compliments.

A: .

C: So. Did he buy you all this booze

A: .

Yes

C: Does he just get you drink whenever you want then

A: Yes

C: Lucky bitch

A: .

C: Will you tell him cheers

A: .

C: From us – tell him thanks from us

A: Sure he'd rather you thanked him yourself.

.

C: I definitely will then.

B: Doesn't he get you drugs now

D: Drugs?

B: Yeah. Drugs. You gave me a whole fucking bag of pills the other day

D: What

C: That's nuts

A: .

C: Where's my bag of pills?

A: I just

D: You Gave 'B' a whole bag of pills? Are you out of your fucking mind

A: I've got loads.

He gives me loads.

B: Sold them to my brother.

D: You're a dick.

B: Even Alan Sugar had to start somewhere pals.

D: Are you Alright?

B: Yeah

D: Not you you Idiot.

'A'. Are you alright?

A: .

Yeah

B: She's Brilliant

C: She's high as a fucking kite she's excellent

D: No, are you actually Alright

B: She Stood up in the middle of Maths yesterday and
Climbed Onto her desk it was hilarious

C: Yeah – and then she

B: For No Reason

C: Yeah – and then she

B: Literally No Fucking Reason

C: Shut up – and then she Climbed out of the shitting window

B: Yeah

C: It was Hilarious

B: Yeah

C: People were talking about it All day

B: Yeah

C: It was Excellent

D: Good for you guys – 'A' you are clearly not alright

B: Don't be boring 'D'

C: Yeah don't be Boring 'D'

A: I'm

Fine

C: See – she's fine

B: She's brilliant

D: My Mum told me not to hang out with you anymore

B: Who? Me?

D: No – with you – with 'A'.

A: .

　　Oh.

C: Which Mum?

D: NAME2

B: The boring one

C: Yeah, that's the boring one

B: Just ignore her

C: She's a bellend

D: She said she sees you.

　　Stumbling around.

　　Spewing into bushes in the park

B: Funny

D: Bad influence.

　　.

　　She says.

B: Boring.

C: Your Mums are boring.

A: .

D: Has he done More than look at your tits?

　　.

　　*A shrugs.*

D: Do you even remember?

　　*A shrugs.*

D: What about his mates?

*A shrugs.*

D: You're not alright.

You are definitely not alright.

.

A: I.

B: Shut up 'D'.

She's brilliant.

Look at her.

She's absolutely brilliant.

## 34. SORRY.

**This scene is between two children (A and B).**

A: I had no idea.

B: It's alright.

A: I am so sorry

B: It's alright

A: I am really really profoundly sorry

B: Got that

A: I Feel Awful – I feel so Awful I'm

B: Calm down

A: Your face is covered in blood

B: That's an exaggeration

A: Nope.

No.

No it's not.

You've got blood coming out of your nose

B: Seemed rude to open the door with a tampon sticking out of it.

.

A: .

I wanted to help.

B: Yes

A: I just wanted to Do something to help

B: I know

A: I wanted to make it better for you – watching it get worse every day was incredibly painful and difficult

B: I'm sorry to hear that, that sounds very hard for you

A: Sorry

B: Look, I'm not sure what you

A: I want to help

B: Yes

A: I really want to help

B: Your helping hasn't turned out to be very helpful.

.

But I do appreciate your effort.

A: I just told my Mum

B: Yes

A: That's all

B: Yes

A: I thought she'd maybe

Adopt you or

B: Don't think it works like that

A: Let you stay at ours for a bit at least

B: You've got about eleven brothers and sisters she's got a lot on her plate

A: Three. There's only three of us.

B: I know.

I was just trying to make one of us feel better.

.

A: I didn't think she'd just march round here and

B: No

A: Have a Go at

B: No

Well

A: That was a really stupid move

B: Not sure there are many Good moves.

A: .

No.

I guess not.

.

I could tell my Dad

B: Not a good idea

A: My Dad is almost as big as him

B: Right

A: He could get him I reckon

B: Get him

A: Yeah like.

Get him.

B: Your Dad ever hit anyone?

A: .

Accidentally. Once. Yeah.

B: Well if he wants to come round and accidentally punch
him in the face that'd be much appreciated.

.

A: Where is he?

B: Walking it off.

A: .

B: This is him holding back a bit.

Probably punching the shit out of a tree right now.

.

A: Where's she?

B: Drinking.

A: What will you do?

B: Not sure.

Nothing To do.

A: .

I'm sorry.

B: I know.

.

Don't cry.

## 35. STORY.

**This scene is between two children or two adults
or one adult (A) and one child (B).**

A: Once upon a time there was a little girl.

.

And this little girl was very little. She was very small
indeed. She was little enough to slip in between
floorboards and down the plughole in the bath and to
sleep in matchboxes vodka's all gone.

all gone.

.

and she did – she slept in matchboxes and she used a
little piece of cotton wool as a pillow and another piece
as a duvet and she'd close the matchbox up tight which
was silly actually which was a bit fucking stupid actually
because some nights, most nights, she'd come really close
to suffocating because there's not much Air in a matchbox.

.

But this little girl didn't mind.

She didn't mind not breathing.

She didn't mind at all.

She was very very very very very very very very tired.

Some mornings, most mornings, she'd wake up with blood round her mouth why are you lying like that. With your arms pinned to you like that. You look like a little squashed beetle.

Are you being like her. Like the little tiny girl in the matchbox with the blood around her mouth.

Some mornings she'd wake up with blood around her mouth and she'd push the matchbox open and she'd wait as long as she possibly could to Gasp for air and then she would, she'd Gasp a lungful and then she'd lie with her arms pinned to her sides like you do and she'd make a low buzzing noise.

Hmmmmmmmmmmmmmmm.

hmmmmmmmmmmmmmmmmmmmm.

like she was a fly.

like she was hoping that all the flies in the house, all the bluebottles that live in the corners of the white cracked windows would come to her in her matchbox and lick the blood off her mouth and start to eat her from the inside out.

hmmmmmmm.

hmmmmmmmmmmmmm.

start to wriggle down her mouth and her windpipe and remember she's very little vodka's all gone so one little bluebottle would block her throat up quite nicely actually, would stop the air getting to her lungs quite perfectly, like a little cork in a bottle and then the other bluebottle would come and they would start to eat her from the inside out perhaps, as all the blood comes pouring up from her stomach and all the black bile and the foam from inside of her comes running up into her mouth the bluebottles could lick it and spit it and drink it and hmmmmm hmmmmm eat it and shit it and drain her and fill her up until she could just stop breathing she could just stop in and out in and out

and then

when they had finished

she could sit up

all bones, just bones now, nice rattly bones

and she could climb out of her matchbox

and go past the fat drunk bluebottles at the white cracked window

and she could climb outside onto the window ledge

and she could jump.

all the way down to the green soft green blue green grass.

and she could smash.

into small pieces.

and she could burrow into the earth.

into the soil.

and she could nearly not exist then.

she could wait for a family to come along and light a
bonfire there.

so that she could turn to ash.

so that she could turn to air.

so that she could turn to nothing.

## 36. PRAM.

**This scene is between two children (A and B).**

*A and B are looking at a pram. A baby is screaming. They stare at it. At
each other. A paces a little. B puts their hands over their ears.*

*They stare at the pram. For a really, really long time.*

*A kicks the pram really fucking hard.*

## 37. DRAWING.

**This scene is between two children (A and B).**

A: She asked me to give this to you

B: Red or green

A: .

    She didn't cry this time

B: I prefer red but if you want red I don't mind.

A: She was a bit fatter

B: .

A: Like she used to be – her arms were a bit podgy and she'd
got her belly back.

B: Red is strawberry and green is apple.

A: Her cheeks were a bit squidgy

B: But that's bollocks really cos both are just sugar basically

A: NAME1 cried

B: I'm going to have the red then.

   If there's no objection.

A: NAME1 did all the crying and I didn't cry at all and she
   was really good, she was fatter and she didn't cry and
   she said she's been going to the Chaplain and she's been
   doing library duty and everyone's been really nice to her
   so that's good.

B: This is rank

A: Don't eat it then.

B: .

A: She asked about you.

B: I cooked dinner

A: Right

B: I burnt dinner

A: Right

B: I ate it all

A: Right

B: And I threw up

A: Right

B: And then I went to the shop

A: Right

B: But I didn't have any money

A: Okay

B: And I had vomit all down my front

A: Gross

B: It hadn't dried yet

A: That's disgusting

B: So I stank

A: Obviously

B: Because it's so hot I really stank

A: That's disgusting

B: I couldn't get to the loo in time

A: You're not Five

B: And I put my hand in the tub

A: Gross

B: The tub with the laces

A: Okay

B: And I was staring at Mr NAME1

A: Weird

B: And he was staring back – just behind the till, just Staring

A: Alright then

B: And I just grabbed a fistful

A: I mean

B: And I just walked off.

.

A: She drew you this.

She said it's You. As a baby. At the beach.

She said she never got to take you.

She said the best she did was stick you in a washing up bowl in the garden but that you loved it. She said she forgot to put a hat on you. And that you burnt until your shoulders blistered. And that she put you in a cold bath. And she pressed the blisters with a dishcloth that she put in the freezer. And that she kissed you. And that she didn't drink until you were sleeping. That she watched you fall asleep. And that the sheets stuck to your blisters. But you didn't cry. Cos you'd learnt not to cry. And that she was a shit Mum. And that she wished she'd just taken you to the beach on a hot day like a Normal Mum. Like Mums are supposed to. And that she draws you. All the time. Cos she's got no pictures of you. She said her wall is covered in pictures of us cos Gran had us and sent pictures but with you no one had you so no one took pictures so there are no pictures to send so she draws you. And that she's so sorry. And that she Did kiss you. She wanted me to tell you that she Did kiss you that time. Soothe. She kept saying Soothe. She wanted me to tell you that that time she did Soothe you. She did watch you. She did feel Close to you, she felt your Closeness and your Smallness, she said, and she did feel – just for a little bit – like a Mum to you but that you deserved to have an Actual Mum all the time and so she draws you in wellies in puddles and on beaches with ice lollies and in school uniforms that are washed and cleaned and hung out on the line to dry so they smell of cotton and summer and she draws you eating melon and she draws you watching telly and she draws you sliding down stairs in sleeping bag covers cos she read that in a book once and that she draws you holding me and holding NAME1 and she draws you sitting in a vegetable patch and at Blackpool and drinking milk and flicking the light switch off and being held in her arms and she draws you drawing and painting and eating and crying and sleeping and dancing and kissing a boy kissing a girl kissing her and I lied actually I lied cos she cried the whole time she cried the Whole time like she always does and I wish you'd come just so maybe she doesn't cry for the Whole time.

.

B: Did you tell her I hated her?

A: .

No.

She was already crying.

B: Did you tell her I thought she was a piece of shit

A: No

B: A waste of space

A: No

B: That I wish she'd drank herself to death before bothering to have kids

A: .

No.

.

B: Will you go again?

A: Yes.

B: Well tell her next time would you.

And tell her she can't draw for shit while you're at it.

## 38. CANAL.

**This scene is between two children (A and B).**

A: I'm not supposed to be here.

.

B: No one's Supposed to be here, it's midnight by a canal.

.

A: Are you alright?

.

Slow down, you'll be sick.

B: Sorry.

.

Haven't eaten for ages.

.

What is it

A: Tuna

B: Stinks

A: You're welcome

B: Thank you. Sorry. I mean it. Thank you.

Just hate fish.

A: Didn't have anything else I could get away with.

Nothing in the fridge.

Mum stockpiles tuna.

In case of the world ending.

She reckons it's Imminent.

Ever since

You know – whatshisface invaded

What's it called.

.

Impending doom.

Tuna and beans.

B: Bring beans next time.

A: Beans in a sandwich?

B: Just the tin.

And a spoon

A: You want a camping stove too

B: Could you

A: Fuck off.

.

Next time?

.

B: Will you.

Will you come again?

A: No ta.

.

It's fucking grim.

What're you even Doing?

B: .

   Don't know.

   .

   Can't go back.

   Not safe.

A: People are worried

B: Bullshit

A: They are.

   .

   Seriously, slow down. You're gagging.

B: I'm freezing.

A: Yeah, cos it's a canal and it's midnight and it's fucking January.

B: Did you bring anything warm

A: No

B: Okay

A: You didn't fucking Ask me to

B: No. It's okay.

A: .

   I'm pissed off with you.

   They're all worried and I have to lie.

B: I'm sorry.

A: I'm worried about you

B: .

A: I think I thought it was a bit funny, but it's not 'B', it's actually not funny at all.

B: .

A: Can't you just come back

B: No.

A: What's your plan

B: I haven't got one

A: That's a bit stupid

B: I know

A: This is worse.

This must be worse than

B: It isn't.

It really, really isn't.

There really, really isn't anything worse than home.

.

I love you.

A: No you don't

B: I do

A: Come back then

B: I really do love you

A: People are asking about you

B: Bullshit

A: It's not

B: Alright. Like who

A: Teachers and stuff.

B: I don't believe you

A: They are

B: Didn't ask about me when I turned up stinking of Piss

A: .

B: Off my face on

A: Alright

B: Whatever I could get my

A: Okay

B: Hands on – I mean

A: Your Dad.

　　Your Dad's asking

B: No he's not.

　　.

　　No he's not asking.

　　As if he's suddenly asking.

A: .

　　Those. Those blokes.

　　Those

B: .

    What d'you tell them.

A: Nothing.

    I

    Nothing.

B: .

A: .

    They put a fucking brick through my window.

B: .

    Sorry.

    .

A: My sister can't sleep at night she's so scared.

B: Sorry.

A: I know.

    .

    Where are you sleeping

B: In the marshes.

    It's warmer in the grass.

    Foxes sleep there.

A: They'll eat your face

    .

    I'm scared.

    It's really dark.

I'm really scared.

I'm really properly scared.

B: I know.

A: .

You can have my coat.

I'm not coming again.

I can't.

But you can have my coat.

### 39. LOVE.

**This scene is for two children or two adults or one adult (A) and one child (B).**

A: I love you

B: No

A: I do

B: No

A: I really love you

B: No thanks

A: I love you

B: No

A: I love your arms

B: No

A: I love your face

B: No

A: I love your neck

B: No

A: I love the way you look when you're really angry

B: No

A: Like now

B: No

A: Or sad

B: No

A: Like now

B: No

A: I love it when you're eating – you eat in the most
Beautiful way

B: No

A: You start by eating really sort of Daintily like you're really
aware you're being watched and you're Trying to make it
beautiful

B: No

A: And then you just get carried away by the actual food and
you Go To Fucking Town and you Hoover

B: No

A: Like you've not eaten in Years

B: No

A: Maybe you haven't

B: No

A When you eat like that – maybe you haven't eaten in years

B: No

A: The way that you eat a Tuna sandwich

B: No

A: Is perfection

B: No

A: I love how you are with animals

B: No

A: With people

B: No

A: With rocks

B: No

A: And nature

B: No

A: And Cars

B: No

A: And vehicles in general, I love how you are on a Bike

B: No

A: It is a Beautiful thing to watch you Mount a Bike

B: No

A: I love it when you dance

B: No

A: Dance for me

B: No

A: You let your hair fall loose

B: No

A: And you close your eyes

B: No

A: In a reverie

B: No

A: Do you know what Reverie means

B: Nope

A: Do you want to

B: no

A: Your hands on your waist

B: No

A: Your elbows

B: No

A: Your hands on your pants

B: No

A: Pulling them down

B: No

A: Letting me pull them down

B: No

A: Is hands down the most beautiful thing on the planet

B: No

A: Please stop saying No

B: No.

No.

A: It's making me want to hate you when I just want to love you.

## 40. NIGHT.

### This scene is for one child (A) and a baby or one adult and a baby.

*It is nighttime.*

*A holds her baby and sings it back to sleep.*

## 41. HIT.

### This scene is for two children or two adults or one child (B) and one adult (A).

*A and B sit. There is music on – loud. They drink. They take drugs. They dance. They sit down. They dance. They kiss. A kisses B hard. B pushes A away. A kisses B harder. B starts to try to hit A. A kisses harder. B pushes A off. B dances as hard and as fast as they can.*

## 42. CAR.

**This scene is for two children (A and B).**

A: I got this for you.

B: I don't want it.

A: I did it for you

B: I didn't ask you to

A: I know you didn't but I still did it For you

B: That's fucking stupid cos not only do I not Want it I am pissed off you Did it.

A: .

Well that's ungrateful

B: You stole a car

A: Which was no small effort

B: You Stole a fucking car

A: Which is a big fucking deal

B: And then you Drove said stolen car

A: Again – not an inconsiderable effort given that I do not drive

B: And made me get in it

A: Legally – I do not drive legally – I drive brilliantly. Just unofficially.

And you were Invited.

I Invited you.

I Invited you to get in it.

There was no Made – no one Made you.

I don't recall getting out of the fucking car, lifting your fat arse up and then pushing you Into the car at at fucking Gunpoint or something.

Think I pulled up, beeped the horn like an absolute G, rolled down the window like a motherfucking legend and said

Hey 'B'. Get in.

Not an instruction.

An Invitation.

.

B: It's a shit car

A: I didn't feel I could be picky.

.

B: I'm cold.

.

A: I thought you said you were Bored.

.

B: I Am fucking bored.

.

I didn't expect you to Do anything about it.

A: .

Surprised?

B: Uh

   Yeah

A: Surprised I can be so

B: shut up

A: Romantic

B: gonna be sick

A: So

B: Shut up

A: Spontaneous

B: You're a prick

A: I mean

B: A massive prick

A: But are you a bit not bored right now.

B: .

A: Are you a bit the opposite of fucking bored right now?

B: .

A: So was it quite a good idea.

B: .

A: Have some vodka.

B: .

A: Have some vodka, have a fag and put your feet up and I'll drive you really far away and we can have an adventure. Like. A proper fucking adventure.

## 43. COFFEE.

**This scene is between two children (A and B).**

A: I got you a coffee.

B: .

A: I didn't know what to get.

.

Chocolate didn't seem

Right

Somehow – it seemed like a more serious thing was required.

Given that you're covered in blood.

And this is a hospital.

And I don't know what to do.

And

The only time I was in a hospital is when my brother fell off a climbing frame and all his teeth fell out and my Dad drank about six coffees and punched a wall.

.

Maybe I should punch a wall.

Maybe that would make you feel better.

Maybe that would make Me feel better.

Bit of wall punching.

I mean.

It was awful.

When he did it.

My Mum sort of cried and put her whole hand over
her face and kept going NAME1 how could you this is
so Embarrassing, I'm so Embarrassed NAME1, but my
brother – I think my brother found it kind of comforting
and Nice, maybe Nice to have the violence um sort
of Displaced somehow, contained somewhere else or
something and also Also there was something about
how Extreme his – my Dad I mean, I'm talking about
my Dad – there was something really comforting about
how Angry he was, about the Violence and Extremity of
his emotion, even though it was really properly bloody
embarrassing, it was sort of lovely to know that he Cared
that much that he didn't know what to do except drink six
coffees and punch a wall.

So.

I could punch a wall for you

B: No

A: No.

No.

Bad idea.

.

I Do care though.

.

I Do really want you to know that I care enough to do that
for you.

.

B: I don't drink coffee

166

A: Nope.

Me neither.

## 44. EMERGENCY.

**This scene is for one child (A).**

*A is on the phone.*

A: Ambulance – I I I I need

Ambulance

And

Police – I.

.

Please.

Please help.

.

Oh God.

It's.

.

It's my Mum it's.

.

It's my.

.

Can you come quickly please? I don't know what to do.

## 45. WARM.

**This scene is between two children or two adults
or one child (A or B) and one adult (A or B).**

A: And?

B: It's warm

A: You're lying

B: I'm not

> A I can feel it from here, you're dripping everywhere and
> it's Freezing.

> .

> Stop it – you're spraying everywhere.

> .

> Get a towel, you'll freeze.

B: .

> I like it.

> .

> It's lovely.

> .

> It's all warm.

> .

> All this Sun.

> On my Skin.

> And the water.

All Big and Cold and Frightening and making each breath shorter

Each

Breath

Count.

.

And then I looked towards you.

.

On the beach.

.

Sitting like a little word on a page a blue mark against a bluer sky, not moving.

Constant and steady and There.

.

I could bob my head under and fill my lungs with sea water and then I could come back up and open my eyes and you were there.

Just as before.

Looking at me.

Looking at me looking at you.

I could almost feel your breath against my arm or my neck or my cheek. Warm.

.

And it made my whole face ache.

And it made my whole heart ache.

And my knees buckle.

And my body head inwards.

And I felt Held.

All the way out there at sea.

I felt Held.

# Adult / Child Scenes.

## 46. AMBULANCE 1.

**This scene is between one child (C) and
two adults (A and B) or three adults.**

A: Okay, can you hear me?

Can you just sit up a second for me?

B: That's great, can you look straight ahead?

That's great, and can you tell me your name?

C: 'C'

B: Fantastic, that's fantastic.

Okay, and can you tell me what day it is?

C: Wednesday.

A: Brilliant.

B: Well done sweetheart.

And can you tell me where you are?

C: Home.

A: That's right.

That's right.

B: Well done.

Well done sweetheart.

A: That's great.

B: Keep your eyes open

C: trying

A: I know you are – you need to try as hard as you possibly can

C: trying

B: Well done sweetheart, that's great. You're doing great. You're doing really great.

## 47. MAGNOLIA.

**This scene is between an adult (A) and a child (B), or could be between two adults, with a younger person playing B.**

A: .

I love it here at night.

B: I know.

A: It's

So

Quiet.

B: .

A: I always come out here on first nights.

I'm so jittery.

Excited and panicked and impatient.

NAME1 is so much better, so much calmer. Steadier.

B: You don't say.

A: I'd want to watch you all sleeping. Check each rise and each fall of each breath.

One boy – I'd been watching him sleep, he was so little and so quiet – he must've been about seven – and I was leaning against the door watching him, just enjoying being near him, enjoying the constancy of the tangible fact that he was still Alive when, without opening an eye he said – Stop Fucking Watching Me You Psycho Bitch.

.

After that, we agreed I'd come out here and NAME1'd stay inside til I'd calmed down a bit.

.

That boy. Psycho bitch boy – he's an Art teacher now. Married. Kids. He comes round on a Sunday sometimes.

B: I know.

His name is NAME2.

A: Of course you know.

.

I thought I'd get better. Hundreds of kids. And still I have to hide out out here.

B: I know.

A: .

I wish you weren't leaving.

B: Thank you for having me

A: Don't

B: Thank you for looking after me

A: For God's sake don't do that

B: I want to say thank you.

A: I don't want you to.

I just think of you as ours and when you say thank you it means you don't.

B: .

I'm not yours.

A: I know.

.

B: I'm not yours not even a little bit.

A: I know.

.

B: I'd have liked to have been.

But I'm not.

A: No.

No, you're not.

.

We'll sell this place soon.

Go and live on a Greek island.

Get a little flat in London. Go to Galleries and exhibitions.

B: No you won't.

A: No.

We won't.

He's dying. NAME1 is. He's actually dying.

B: I know.

A: I'm sad.

B: I know.

A: That's a Magnolia tree.

B: I know.

A: It only flowers for One Week

B: I know.

A: Isn't that incredible

B: Yes.

A: You tend to it for a whole year and then it only blooms for a week.

B: Yes.

A: But it's so so so So beautiful for that week.

B: Yes.

A: .

When we got married my dress was called Magnolia White.

B: That's nice.

A: Isn't it.

B: .

A: You Hated us when you got here.

B: No.

A: You did.

B: No. I was just sad.

.

A: I wish you'd stay.

B: No you don't.

I get to go back to my Mum.

That's a Good Thing.

A: She doesn't deserve you.

B: .

A: Maybe I'll sell. When he's gone.

.

B: He's not leaving for a trip. He's fucking dying. His lungs are black.

A: .

Yes.

.

That was an awful thing to say. What I said. About your Mum. Not deserving you.

.

.

I couldn't have loved you anymore than I do. Than I have. Than I will.

B: I know.

## 48. SMILEY FACE.

**This scene is for a child (A) and an adult (B).**
**The adult can be offstage – their voice just played.**
**Or – the adult's text could be removed.**

*There is a camera. Recording. The child looks directly into it for a long time.*

A: Will he be able to see me?

B: Yes. On a monitor.

A: Okay.

And that's.

I can't.

Right.

Sorry, can I have a glass of water?

.

*Someone brings her one.*

.

Thank you.

B: Okay?

*A nods.*

B: Can you tell me when you first met the defendant – NAME1?

A: On the 13th of November.

B: You're sure about that?

A: Yes.

It was at a party. At my friend's party.

B: Your friend?

A: Yes. NAME2. It was not. He hadn't Decided to have a party. He had an empty house – his parents weren't there. They'd not been there for a while I think. Some people from my school – NAME3 and and NAME4, turned up and sort of persuaded him to have a party I think.

B: You think?

A: No, I know. He called me – NAME2 called me. He was quite upset. He didn't have very many friends – he was being bullied basically and he called me and I went and we got a bit drunk.

B: Did your parents know you were there?

A: My Mum – I live with my Mum. No. She didn't know I'd gone. I climbed out of my window.

B: Did you do that often?

A: No. That was the first time. I cut my knee.

B: So you walked to the party?

A: He lives on the next street – it took me about two minutes to walk there and when I got there it was Heaving with people. It took me ages to find him.

B: And what did you do?

A: We got drunk. Me and NAME2. I drank a lot. I drank a lot of vodka.

B: Did you do that often?

A: Get drunk?

B: Yes.

A: No. That was only the second time I'd been drunk. My Mum is quite strict. My Aunt is an alcoholic. My Mum doesn't drink.

B: And how did you meet the defendant?

A: Some of us were in the garden. I'd been sick. I'd lost my shoes. We were in the front garden. Someone was passing round a joint.

B: A joint?

A: Weed.

B: And did you smoke some?

A: Yes.

B: A lot?

A: No.

It made me feel sick.

Maybe two tokes

B: Tokes

A: Drags.

.

There were all these Guys suddenly there on the grass. I was sitting on something – some uh – some broken glass. I'd cut myself and I hadn't noticed.

B: Your knee?

A: I'd cut my knee earlier. Then I had this cut on my thigh. The grass was turning red. This guy. Who I later found out was NAME1 sat next to me. He helped me clean my leg up. My jeans were ripped. He gave me some water. And then some more vodka. His friend was making jokes.

B: What kind of jokes.

A: Joking that he was going to

Like

To Kiss me or or

B: Yes?

A: Or to

Or.

To touch me

B: Is that what he said?

A: Finger me. He used the words finger me.

And. NAME1 was really kind. He was really kind.

Sorry.

B: It's okay.

A: He told him to shut up. NAME1 did. Told him to leave me alone. He stroked my hair a bit. Told me I had nice eyes. That I seemed clever. No one tells me I'm clever. I used to think I was quite clever and then no one tells you you are and you stop thinking it so it was nice, it was really nice he told me he thought I was clever.

.

I told him I had a sister. And a little brother. And that my Nan lived round the corner. And that I'd snuck out.

He walked me home.

Carried me home the last bit.

Wiped my face with his sleeve.

He helped me sneak back in. Gave me a leg up, let me stand on his shoulders. The dog was barking.

Told me to drink water.

He wrote his number on the bottom of my stomach and a smiley face.

.

When I got home I took all my clothes off and I looked at that number and that smiley face in the mirror for a long time and then I wrote the number in my phone.

.

And I just looked at it.

For ages.

.

And then I texted him.

B: And what did you text him.

A: A smiley face. Just a smiley face.

## 49. FARM.

**This scene is between one adult (B) and one child (A).**

A: An actual farm

B: Yep

A: Pigs and cows

B: Yep

A: Sheep and chickens

B: Yep

A: Ducks and geese

B: Mmm

A: Goats

B: Sure

A: Sure?

B: If you like.

A: .

Is it a farm?

B: Yes

A: An actual one?

B: Yes

A: Do you promise?

B: Yes.

A: Do you promise promise?

B: Yep

A: Cross your heart and hope to

B: Die, yes.

A: Okay.

I like farms.

B: Yes

A: I like animals

B: Yes

A: Will it be dark when we get there

B: Yes

A: So I won't See the animals straight away

B: Nope

A: But I'll see them the next day

B: Yep

A: And I'll hear them

B: Maybe

A: Maybe

B: They'll be sleeping. So you might not hear them straight
   away.

A: Right.

   Right.

   And.

B: Yes

A: If I don't like it there

B: You will

A: But if I Don't

B: You just Will

A: But If I don't then I can just leave.

B: .

   You'll like it

A: I can just Up and leave

B: You'll love it

A: I can just fuck right off.

   Like I always do.

   Like I have done.

B: I'll just come and get you again

A: Yeah but

B: And you won't need to

A: Right

B: Cos you'll like it

A: Right

B: Cos you'll really love it

A: Right

B: Cos it'll feel like Home.

   And everyone'll be lovely to you.

   And there'll be loads of fluffy animals to play with.

A: Right.

   .

   And if not. If not. I'll just fuck off again.

   And soon.

   Soon.

   You'll just get bored of looking.

## 50. HOME BIRD.

**This scene is for one child (A) and one adult (B).**
**B's text can be removed or recorded.**

*It is to camera – A is being filmed for a documentary. Obviously, you can do this with or without a camera.*

A: So this is my room.

.

I didn't choose this colour, this was just what was here before cos uh cos we haven't had time to paint it oooor

Anything yet but I don't mind much I sort of think it's okay – I've put stickers up and

I'm used to moving quite a bit – we've moved house lots, my Mum doesn't like staying in one place very long. Itchy feet she says. I'm – my Nan calls me – a Home Bird.

.

I was born at home – I was really quick. And Nan says I just wanted to be at home so I hurried right up so I could just stay put.

.

So. I sort of hope we stay here for a while. Cos it'd be nice to be in one place I think. Even though. Even though it's a bit um um Sad I guess cos Mum isn't – Not Sad – I don't think I Feel Sad that she's not here.

.

B: What do you feel?

A: .

*Smiles.*

*Shrugs.*

Don't know.

.

Think I just feel that it's nice to sort of

Uh

Sort of Be in one place for a bit and that

.

My Mum's really fun and she's a really loud person and. She was always. She. My friends at other schools and stuff – my friends have always – I don't really get to have friends cos we're moving so I don't Mean friends, but – my Friends or or people I've hung out with for a bit – they are always really Jealous because she's the one letting us drink or giving us fags or telling us how to

.

B: How to?

A: *Smiles.*

*Shrugs.*

Kiss boys or.

Cheat in exams or.

That you shouldn't worry about next weeks or tomorrows or next years cos Now is here.

.

B: And how does that make you feel?

A: *Smiles.*

*Shrugs.*

I mean.

That's fun isn't it.

That Is fun.

.
.

It's just nice if your Mum does worry about the tomorrows sometimes.

.

They've got pigs here.

And a goat.

And the chicks were born last week and I named one.

B: What did you name it?

A: *Smiles.*

NAME1.

B: .

That's a nice name.

A: *Smiles.*

*Shrugs.*


## 51. MCDONALDS.

### This scene is between an adult (A) and two children (B and C).

*A car.*

*The two children sit on their own for a long time. C is crying. B holds their hand. They stare straight ahead.*

*A enters.*

A: Okay.

B: .

A: Alright.

B: .

A: Now. 'B'. 'NAME1'.

B: 'C'. Her name is 'C'.

A: Right

B: Not 'NAME1'.

A: Got it.

'C'

Sorry.

C: .

A: Are you hungry?

B: No.

A: Thirsty?

B: No.

A: We could drive round to McDonalds

B: We're not allowed McDonalds

A: No.

Me neither.

B: Are you making a joke about your wife or husband not allowing something to make us feel better?

A: .

   Yes.

B: Sounds like you're in a controlling relationship.

A: .

   I'm not in a relationship.

   It was a bad joke.

B: And a lie.

A: That's a strong word

B: But the right word

A: I

B: You were lying about being in a relationship

   In order to encourage us to talk.

A: You're not under investigation.

   I'd like you to feel comfortable. That was my motivation.

B: So you lied

A: I apologise.

B: Why would you Lie in order to make us feel Comfortable?

   That's a really odd tactic.

   I now completely distrust you.

   .

A: Right.

   I'm very sorry.

   I am currently divorcing my wife.

I cheated on her.

B: .

And you're telling us this because

A: Because I thought I'd try being very very honest instead.

.

B: I've tried McDonalds. It's rank. It's cow floor sweepings.
I don't feel I'm losing anything by not being allowed it
thanks.

A: Got it.

B: We'd like to go back inside please.

A: Okay.

You understand that we can't do that.

Not right now.

B: .

A: We need to go to where I work.

B: The police station.

A: Yes.

We've called your Aunt. NAME2.

She's going to come and meet us there and we're going to
have a chat and go through everything.

B: We'd like to go home.

A: I understand. But that's not going to be possible for a little
while.

B: I'm not thick. We're not thick.

A: I don't think you are.

B: You're talking to us like you do.

A: I'm just trying to be clear.

What happened in there was very, very serious.

B: Yeah, we got that.

Don't start the car.

.

I'd like a lawyer.

A: .

You're not in any trouble.

B: It's our right. To have a lawyer.

A: We can talk about that.

B: You shouldn't even be talking to us without an appropriate adult.

A: .

Your Aunt is going to meet us at the station.

B: You already said that.

I'd like to go back inside now.

A: That's not possible.

B: Because it's a crime scene.

A: .

Yes.

B: How long until we can go back?

A: I can't say, I'm afraid.

B: My Aunt lives a long way away. We need to be able to go to school.

A: We can talk about that.

B: We'll need to be able to visit my Mum.

A: And that.

B: We grew up round here. All our friends are here. C's best friend lives just across the road. We'd like to stay put.

A: I understand.

B: You do?

A: I think so

B: Doubt it.

    .

    Is he dead?

A: We can talk about that at the station.

B: Or now. We could just talk about that now.

A: .

    No. No, he's not dead.

B: He crawled out of the house

A: Yes

B: There was blood everywhere

A: Yes.

    .

B: He might, mightn't he? He might die?

She got him right near his heart didn't she?

And she really pushed it.

All the way in.

She was Screaming her head off.

So she might have killed him actually, mightn't she?

He might actually die. Mightn't he?

A: .

Yes. Yes, he might.

B: .

Good.

I hope he does.

## 52. SCAR.

**This scene is between an adult (A) and a child (B).**

A: Come here

Put your feet up here. Give them here.

Come on.

Let me warm them a bit.

You're freezing.

B: The heating's off.

A: Is it?

B: .

Yeah

A: Who did that?

B: What

A: Turned it off

B: .

    You did.

    It's been off for ages.

    Can't afford it. You said. NAME1 said.

A: .

    Got any money in your piggy bank?

B: I haven't got a piggy bank.

A: You used to.

B: .

A: Turn the telly on if you like.

B: It's on.

A: Is it?

B: Yes.

A: Can't hear it.

B: You told me to turn it down.

A: I didn't.

    I didn't.

    I wouldn't do that little one.

    You can turn it up.

B: You're shouting

A: I'm not.

Stop being so horrid.

B: .

A: Are you hungry?

B: No.

A: You sure?

B: Yes.

A: NAME1'll be back soon. He'll make you something.

B: I don't want him to.

A: Be nice.

B: I don't want him to make me anything.

A: Be nicer to him.

He'll go if you're a brat.

Don't ruin it 'B'.

Don't ruin it for me.

For us.

It's good he's here.

He's nice, isn't he?

You like him.

B: I don't.

A: You do.

He likes you.

B: I don't like him.

A: You do.

Go on.

You do a bit.

Those big arms.

He gives good hugs, doesn't he?

He gives nice kisses.

B: Stop it.

A: He does though.

　　·

Bit loud.

　　·

You like me being happy, don't you?

You like it when I'm happy.

It's nicer then, isn't it?

God, when I'm sad.

I can be a right grump, can't I?

I can be a right misery.

When I won't get up.

It's been better since he's been around, hasn't it?

We went for dinner. To a Restaurant.

B: To a Carvery.

A: That's a restaurant.

That counts.

B: I'm a vegetarian.

A: They do salad.

    You had a nice salad.

    And that pasta thing.

    And a coke.

    He paid for it.

    He left a Tip.

B: He put some shrapnel in a jar.

A: That counts.

B: No it doesn't

A: Says who

B: He put about six coppers in there. And a Euro

A: A Euro's quite a lot nowadays – that's bloody generous

B: It's Not

A: You're such a fucking Brat.

    Don't be such a bitch 'B'.

B: .

A: You can be a right bitch when you want to be.

    When you want to ruin everything.

    Put your feet back.

    Don't sulk.

    It's horrid when you sulk.

    You ruin it.

We're having a nice time watching telly and you're being a right fucking pain.

.

Make me a cup of tea.

B: No.

A: Go on.

B: No.

A: Go on.

B: No. I don't want to.

A: .

NAME1'll be here in a minute.

He'll make me a tea.

B: And throw it in your face again.

A: He didn't do that.

B: Yes he did.

A: I'd be covered in burns if he did that.

B: What's that on your fat tummy then?

A: Nothing.

B: It's a fucking scar.

A: Don't swear.

Don't swear at me.

I've had that forever.

I've had that for Years.

That's nothing to do with him.

Don't be such a bitch.

Don't be such a cunt.

You're such a cunt.

You're such a fucking cunt.

You're so fucking nasty.

You came out fucking nasty.

Screaming constantly.

Always whining.

Always being a right fucking bitch.

Get your feet off me.

They're fucking freezing.

## 53. MINUTES AND SECONDS.

**This scene is between one adult (A) and one child (B).**

*They sit for a long time.*

A: Are you okay?

B: .

　　Now?

A: Yes.

　　Now.

B: .

　　This second?

A: Yes.

And

More seconds.

Ideally.

Seconds and minutes around this second – are you okay?

.

B: .

Yes.

I'm okay.

## 54. CRY.

**This scene is between one adult (B) and one child (A).**

A: Don't cry.

B: .

A: Please please don't cry.

.

.

.

A: I'm just. Let me just. If I can just. And then get out of here then. Then I'm. I'll be Gone and.

B: What're you

A: It just seemed more

B: Doing I

A: Straightforward this way – it just seemed

B: Oh my God

A: Easier – I

B: Easier

A: I'm not. I didn't Plan this I

B: oh my god

A: I just. I assumed you'd be

Asleep

B: It's two o'clock in the morning

A: Which is why I assumed you'd be asleep

B: It's literally ten past two in the morning

A: Please don't cry

B: I can't believe you're

A: Please don't cry

B: I'm not going to fucking cry I'm going to fucking scream.

A: .

I don't want it to be like this.

B: Jesus Christ

A: I don't want it to be this way

B: I can't

A: This isn't My Choice – I didn't Choose this

B: Could you shut up could you just shut up really really
quickly I.

A: I'm

B: Acting like this has all just Happened to you.

A: .

B: Acting like you have No Agency in this I.

    I Cannot believe that you.

    .

    I was Asleep. I was fast asleep.

    Your Dad's asleep. Your sister is asleep 'A' – your sister
    is fast asleep upstairs and you are climbing in through
    windows I can't.

A: .

    This seemed easier.

B: Easier.

A: Easier

B: easier

A: Yeah, Easier

B: Easier Than What?

A: Asking

    for Help

B: This is you asking for help

A: d'you know what

B: This is how you ask for help

A: this is not

B: You want my help

A: this was not

B: So you climb in through the / fucking window at two
    o'clock in the morning

A: / a good idea you're you're really

B: I'm really

A: angry you're clearly really / angry

B: / of course I'm Fucking Angry 'A' you're / Climbing In
    Through Windows

A: / okay then I think that you should / just

B: / I'm Angry and I'm Fucking Confused about your /
    methods of Asking for

A: / I didn't – look, I didn't Plan for this

B: What did you plan for then? What was your Plan?

A: .

   I Need Money.

B: .

A: I know you don't want to Hear that I know you want me
   to be climbing in here requesting Rehab help or or a
   fucking Hug kind of Help or Someone's beat me up and I
   want to go to the fucking police Help or or whatever kind
   of maternal shit you – or but but look I But I need some
   Money and I have a Few ways of getting money a Few
   Sure Fire ways of of getting [money] and I know that if
   you Thought about all those ways you'd prefer me to do
   this.

   You would. So.

   I know that makes me a. But. It's fucking true and I. So.

   I am Asking for Help.

B: .

I was just delighted by you.

I thought you were So Wonderful.

It was harder with your sister – I genuinely didn't have that

Rush of love that you're told about – I Liked her but it was just Hard but You.

Oh my God I thought you were Spectacular.

.

You're not Asking. You're Taking.

A: .

You said you'd always help me

B: I'm not sure that you Robbing me is helping anyone 'A'

A: So Help Me

B: .

No.

.

Use one of your other Sure Fire Ways of getting help.

A: .

Are you.

Cos.

Cos That means.

That means.

do you know what That means

B: Yes

A: I don't think you Do Know

B: yes I do

A: .

    what I have to do

B: you don't Have to

A: I Am Fucking Rattling

B: I will drive you to a hospital

A: Fuck You

B: And I will Sit with you and hold your hand and stroke your
    forehead

A: Fuck you harder

B: I will look after you and commit to being here for you

A: Shut up

B: Or you can get out.

A: you

B: window or door, I don't care

A: are unbelievable I.

    I am In Pain

B: I see that.

A: I Am Suffering

B: I want to help

A: Then give me money

B: No.

A: So I'll go and fuck some sweaty old man then?

I'll go and suck some pervert off because you Won't Help Me – that's what you want

B: No

A: So Fucking Help Me

B: I'll drive you to hospital

A: that's not fucking

B: I'll sit with you here

A: Helpful I

B: I will look after you

A: you have No idea

B: that's probably true

A: the amount of Pain I

B: that's definitely true

A: Please.

B: .

A: Please. Please. Please.

B: 'A'

A: It Hurts – please. Please. Please. Please. Please. Please. please. please. please. please. Please. Please.

please.

please.

please.

please.

.

B: No.

A: Please. Please. PleasepleasepleasepleaseFUCKYOUplease

B: 'A'

A: Stop saying my fucking name like that

*A begins to look for money. Or for things that cost money. A makes
a lot of mess. If there is mess to be made.*

B: 'A'

A: I Don't Trust people who say my name on Fucking Repeat
like

B: 'A'

A: Like fucking Cops. And fucking Nurses. And fucking
Teachers and Social Workers and

B: 'A'

A: People who've been given Training on how to
communicate with Difficult Fucking People

B: If we just

A: Get Told to Use people's names All The Time as a Tactic

B: can you not

A: It's like you didn't Birth me it's like I didn't Fall out of your
vagina

B: that's really Valuable can you

A: You have a hole in the crotch of your pyjamas by the way.

B: .

A: There's a hole

B: please don't do / that

A: / right there. In the middle.

B: okay

A: Just in case you're feeling a bit

B: I'm

A: Breezy in that department where is your fucking Money

B: 'A'

A: 'A'. 'A'. 'AAAA'

B: I'm

A: I can literally see Where I fell out of you and I'm just
   Letting you know I can in case that's the source of any

B: I'm

A: Discomfort or – in case that's contributing to any

B: I feel so sad

A: My bones feel Wrong I feel like I've been put together in
   the wrong

B: I feel so profoundly sad

A: Do you know what Rattling Is

B: Please stop doing this

A: This is your fault this is your fucking fault I came out
   wrong

B: I remember when you first came back like this and I
   remember holding your head under a tap a warm tap

trying to give you something Life Giving and kind and because no one gives you a fucking / Manual on

A: / Do Not Say Manual oh jesus fucking christ

B: .

I don't know what to say

A: Say Nothing. You're better when you say Nothing.

B: I'm going to call the police

*A has found money – or something that costs money. Brandishes it. Both careful and careless with it.*

A: Don't bother.

I'm done.

I don't exist for you again, you can forget all about me all over again

B: That is Not what we do

A: It's fine. It's all fine.

I'm going.

Gone.

Goinggoinggone.

## 55. WATER.

**This scene is for one adult (A) and one child (B).**

*A bath or a tub of water.*

*A is wearing a nightdress.*

*B is dressed.*

B: Okay.

In you get.

*A shakes her head.*

Come on.

In you go.

*A shakes her head.*

Here.

Hold my hand.

*A does.*

Squeeze it.

*A does.*

I'm here.

.

In you get.

*A gets in, still holding B's hand, still wearing the nightdress.*

There you go.

Now.

Hold still.

*B washes A, tenderly. One of them sings.*

# Adult Scenes.

**This scene is between two adults. (A and B).**

A: Your face is damp.

B: I need you to write that up

A: That your face is damp

B: No

A: You're dripping

B: Obviously not that bit

A: You look Unwell

B: That's not.

    That's not the.

    I'm just going to.

    I'm just going to sit down.

    .

A: Are you alright

B: Could you get me some water

A: As in

B: I'm fine

A: You look like you're going to

B: I need you to write down what happened

A: Vomit or

B: I need you to say exactly what happened

A: Shit yourself or

B: Okay

A: Have some kind of enormous

B: Right

A: Evacuation out of one of your

B: That's

A: Orifices

B: .

A: Alright?

B: Can you just shut up.

A: .

B: Can you just not say the word Orifices again.

A: Alright.

B: Orifices?

A: Okay

B: Who says the word Orifices?

A: Alright.

B: Jesus

A: Got it.

B: .

I need you to just write down what happened

A: What happened

B: What you witnessed

A: What I witnessed

B: Exactly

A: In there

B: Yes exactly

A: What I Witnessed

B: Between her and me

A: Right

B: With the biting

A: And when you hit her

B: With what she said

A: And when you

B: When she spat

A: When you hit her again

B: When she said about having AIDs

A: When you sat on her

B: For protection

A: For your protection

B: For everyone's protection

A: When you sat on her for everyone's protection

B: For her safety

A: For Her safety

B: Yes exactly

A: Oh

B: Yes

A: Oh

B: Yes

A: When you sat on her Neck for Her safety

B: For everyone's safety

A: But for Her safety – that's what you're saying you want me to say

B: Is there water

A: That was for her protection and everyone's safety – you sitting on her neck

B: That was not –

'A'

That was as a Direct result of her behaviour

A: You want me to write that you sat on her neck because of her behaviour

B: Because that's what happened

A: Right

B: I want you to write that because that's what happened

A: Right

B: Right

A: Right

B: I'm not asking you to fabricate anything

A: Oh

B: Jesus

A: I thought

B: We're just going over what happened – Jesus Christ – what the hell do you think we're Doing

A: Well I

B: And – what the fuck – you're prepared to just start Fabricating shit if a senior officer Tells you to

A: No – I just – I'm trying / to Clarify

B: / We're going over what Happened – we're Clarifying what happened

A: And what happened was you Sat on her because of her behaviour

B: Yes

A: And her behaviour was her spitting

B: Yes

A: You sat on her because she spat

B: Because she spat and used threatening language and gestures

A: Gestures

B: Yes exactly

A: Okay

B: Okay

A: Okay

B: Great.

A: .

Sorry, 'B', just to be clear, what is a threatening gesture?

B: .

I feel like you're

A: Sorry

B: Is there some problem

A: Sorry, no

B: Because she just threatened me

A: Right

B: And I acted to protect all of us

A: I'm trying to get a clear idea of what

B: I followed protocol and guidance in order to protect all of us

A: Right

B: And she's fine and I feel pretty shaken up so really

A: Right

B: I could use your support here

A: I didn't feel I needed protection from her.

.

B: She's a drug user.

A: Yes.

B: We're very familiar with her.

A: Yes.

B: You're new.

A: Yes.

B: She's been threatening before.

A: She seemed upset to me.

B: You're new.

A: Yes.

B: She's a pain in the fucking ass

A: I can see that

B: She was threatening. I felt threatened.

A: She stole Tampax. And nappies. And a baby gro.

B: And about eighty quids worth of make up to flog

A: Yes but

B: Not buts – don't wilfully ignore the whole picture because you feel Emotional about the fact she's a Mum

A: I don't feel I'm behaving emotionally

B: You're ignoring fairly critical information to focus on the more emotional aspects of the crime

A: I'm trying to look at the whole picture

B: Are you suggesting that I'm not

A: No, I

B: You're new

A: I would never

B: You're very new

A: Yes, but that's

B: Are you implying I'm not doing my job

A: No – No

B: I felt under threat

A: I

B: I felt like we were in a dangerous situation

A: Well

B: I'm explaining to you that I felt very unsafe

A: So you Beat Her Up and Sat on her Neck and she's about
   half your size and scared and off her face on smack and
   dirt fucking Poor.

   .

   Sorry.

   I'm sorry.

   That was.

   I'm sorry.

B: And that's what you're going to

   .

A: .

   No.

   Yes.

   No.

   I don't.

   No.

   No.

# 57. ARMS.

**This scene is between two adults (A and B).**

A: The kids

B: Asleep

A: Already

B: They're exhausted – you fully tired them out

A: Thought I heard screams insisting the opposite

B: Every Single Night

A: Have I chopped this small enough

B: Nope.

    Do you want wine?

A: .

B: What?

A: Nothing

B: didn't Look like nothing

A: It was fucking nothing

B: .

    Wow

A: Wine would be Great

B: right

A: If you're having some

B: Obviously I am having some you can See I am having some

A: Yes great thanks great

B: She falls asleep standing up. She screams her head off, she hammers her fists on the side of the cot and she shouts NoSleepNoSleepNoSleep little ball of fucking Fury And Fucking Devil Shit Human and then she suddenly

Just

Drops

Spread Eagle on the bed.

Like

An

Angel

And off she goes.

A: Better?

B: It'll do

A: Basil?

B: On the windowsill.

A: Dying.

B: Be alright. Pick from the top.

.

A: All that sea air

B: Killing my basil?

A: No.

Why the kids are so tired. Sea air and Loads and Loads of chips.

B: D'you mind if I smoke

A: Your house

B: You're in it

A: If I say no would it stop you

B: I'd go outside

A: Then no.

.

B: Aren't you going to ask me

A: Ask you what

B: Why I'm so

A: Why you're so

B: Why I'm so

    *Smiles.*

    Why I'm So

    You know

A: Nope

B: Why I'm so

A: Is he sleeping

B: .

    Didn't I say

A: No

B: Quiet as a mouse.

A: Sea air.

B: He always goes like that.

.

Don't I seem different?

A: .

Not specially.

B: I Feel different

A: Okay

B: I feel Happy.

Really

Happy.

A: Okay.

B: Can't you tell?

A: Hadn't noticed any change.

B: Liar.

I didn't get out of bed last time you were here.

A: Not true. You weren't Here last time I was here.

B: .

Okay

A: Last time I came here I came here because your boy your
little Boy Called me

B: Alright

A: He called me from a fucking Pay Phone cos you weren't
paying phone / bills at the

B: / Yeah yeah yeah yeah okay

A: time – With money he'd Nicked from a boy at school –
   nearly peed his / pants

B: / Yes alright

A: He got Smacked in the face for / that

B: / Yes I fucking Know Alright I Get it

A: .

B: Punishing me

A: Maybe you deserve to be a bit punished.

.

B: I beat myself up about it Every Single Day.

.

A: You Just said you were in bed. You Just said you were in
   bed last time I was here. When actually you had pissed off
   and left those two on their own.

   Forgetting that information doesn't sound like you give
   yourself too hard a time.

   .

   What d'you think?

B: Needs salt.

.

A: I'm happy you're happy.

B: .

   I'm not going outside. It's fucking freezing.

A: Okay

B: It's going to snow later

A: No it's not

B: Feels like it

A: Put a coat on then

B: I'll open a window

A: Okay

B: I'll stand by the door

A: Alright

B: It's my house

A: Yes

B: You're judging

A: You're projecting

B: That's so irritating

A: Is it burning?

B: That's so incredibly irritating

A: Is it though?

B: Don't you cook

A: No

B: You used to

A: No

B: You did – you made my tea every night for years

A: And now I don't do it anymore.

No point cooking for just yourself.

B: I met someone.

A: I think it's burning a bit.

B: Turn it down then.

A: Tastes alright

B: Good

A: Just catching a bit.

B: Turn it right down then.

.

I can't stop smiling.

.

He is

So

Tall.

His name is NAME1.

NAME1.

Good, isn't it?

I mean, who'd've thought I'd be with a NAME1.

.

His Arms. I mean. If I could just stop and describe his
Arms to you –

.

A: How d'you turn your oven on?

B: Turn the fucking nob.

A: .

   Does he have kids?


   .


   Does he

B: Yes, loads. Load of them. Twelve of them.

A: .

B: No, he has no kids. Is that a requirement?

A: Does he know You have kids?

B: You said not to introduce any Partners to the kids until it
   had been about six months – you Specifically said

A: You should still Tell fucking partners about the existence of
   said fucking kids

B: We haven't had sex yet, he doesn't need to know I have
   kids

A: You've definitely had sex with him

B: .

A: As If you haven't had sex with him

B: .

   Barely.

A: How do you Barely have sex with someone

B: You just lean back a bit and

A: Okay.

B: Serious voice now

226

A: Hang on.

B: Very very serious voice now

A: Did you tell him you Didn't have children?

B: .

   .

Don't be cross.

I like him.

A: .

Your bulb has gone.

B: Is that a metaphor?

A: This one. How long has it been out – you need to keep on top of things –

B: You'd like him

   .

You'd really like him.

A: I already don't like him.

I like you.

I like your kids.

B: .

His Arms though –

A: Great. You found a man with fucking arms congratulations 'B'

B: Don't be a twat

A: Hasn't it been difficult enough?

Hasn't Everything you've been through

Been difficult enough?

B: .

I really like him.

A: Then why haven't you told him about your children?

B: I am a Whole Human Being I am not just a Mother.

I would like an existence Outside of being just a Mother.

A: Haven't you had enough of that already?

B: .

A: Haven't you had a Shit Ton of that

Already?

## 58. RECORD.

**This scene is between two adults (A and B).**

A: .

B: So, you can sit here

A: .

B: And I'll just sit here

A: .

B: And then when you're ready, I'll hit record

A: .

B: And you can read the letter – or

A: I haven't got a letter

B: Great. That's fine

A: I haven't written a letter

B: That's absolutely fine

A: You didn't say I had to write

B: No

A: a letter, you didn't

B: No

A: tell me I needed to Write

B: No, that's fine

A: I'm not

B: No, that's absolutely fine

A: I'm not Good at

B: No, no problem

A: I didn't know I had to

B: That's not a problem

A: Write something

B: There is no Had to

A: I've done it wrong

B: No

A: I've already got it wrong

B: Not at all

A: I should go and write a letter and do it later

B: No

A: You think I'll sound stupid

B: I think you'll sound brilliant

A: I don't want to get it wrong

B: You won't

A: I can't get it wrong

B: That's not what this is about

A: She won't read my letters

B: She's upset

A: No

B: Well

A: No. She's not Upset.

B: She probably Is upset 'A'.

A: No. 'B'. No. NAME1 is not upset.

She's devastated. I've completely devastated her. She's so small and I've managed to rip her up.

It's like I've declared war on her little bones.

She's War Torn. Famine and fucking wreckage, I've wrecked her cities and bombed her land and her seas and her skies. I have Detonated them. I have caused a Nuclear explosion inside her. She's Fucking Chernobyl. That Thing I held. That Bundle. That Squashed Pile of limbs and features and Screams and Shit that I was supposed to just Grow as best I could – I fucking Ruined her.

.

How do you Devastate a child?

They're supposed to be full of joy.

She has never been full of joy.

She has never had even the smallest amount of joy in her.

She has always just been Sad.

Really, really, really, really, really, really, really, really
Sad.

I did that.

.

B: You're doing something now

A: I'm recording a tape.

B: Yes.

A: I'm putting my voice on tape.

B: Yes.

A: Like when they're in the womb and you talk to them so
they get to know your voice.

B: Yes. Like that.

A: Except I didn't. Because I cared more about Him. Or
him. Or him. Or drink. Or him. Or drugs. Or him. Than
her. So I never fucking talked to that bump. Sometimes
I forgot about it. Sometimes I punched the shit out of
it. Sometimes I got punched. Sometimes I Squeezed
it. Sometimes I Used it. To get Shit. To get Help. Or
Sympathy. Or cash for a fucking BJ –

Do You Know that there are men out there whose Thing is
fucking pregnant women?

Who Want to be sucked off by a Pregnant Woman?

Eight months pregnant. Ding ding ding ding ding.

I did not fucking sing to her so she could know my voice.

B: .

It's not that simple.

A: That's what people like you always say.

B: .

Maybe we always say things like that for a reason.

Because they're true.

.

These things come in cycles. You're trying to break it for her. No one did that for you.

A: I still made choices. I still put her last.

B: .

You can't do anything about any of that.

Not now.

There is nothing you can do about that.

But you can do this.

A: I don't think I can.

B: You have to.

It isn't for you.

A: She's putting up walls.

Perhaps she's better that way.

B: I think it is easier for you to think that

A: No.

I think it's the truth. And I think if you admitted that your little heart would break and your whole fucking value system falls to pieces.

Maybe I don't like her that much.

Maybe that's the whole point.

Maybe that series of choices I made were the right choices and she'll be better off and I'll be better off and that's it.

Maybe I'm just not that fucked about it all.

Maybe I was too off my face the whole time to have created anything resembling A Bond with that girl anything resembling Depth with that girl – anything that looks like a fucking Real Relationship with that girl, who frankly, the only connection we have is that I Managed Somehow not to fucking Kill her inside me, Birthed her in a Haze of Drugs and Pain and Misery and then ignored her for two years till I ended up here.

.

So maybe there's nothing to salvage.

So maybe there's nothing to save.

So maybe I'm done.

Maybe I'm properly done.

## 59. SALT.

**This scene is between two adults (A and B).**

A: This is nice.

B: .

A: It's nice to cook for you.

Thank you for letting me cook for you.

B: Okay.

A: It's really nice

B: Okay

A: It means a lot

B: It's pasta

A: Yes.

It's just pasta

B: I didn't mean just

A: It's fine

B: I know it is but I didn't Say just pasta, I said it's pasta

A: Yes

B: I was identifying it

A: Okay.

B: I was Naming it

A: Okay

B: I was looking down at my bowl and going:

Pasta.

A: Okay.

B: Okay.

A: I know you're busy.

B: It's okay.

A: Can't get over how Tall you are.

B: Okay.

A: I'm not very tall.

B: .

A: Your Dad was quite tall.

B: Right.

A: Does it taste okay

B: Yes

A: I put salt in

B: Yep

A: And then I thought maybe you don't like salt

B: No

A: Or maybe you're very healthy – you look very healthy

B: No

A: And salt isn't Good for you, is it

B: Not too much, no

A: But it's okay

B: It's okay

A: It's just okay

B: I didn't say Just. It's okay

A: I'm sorry

B: It tastes fine.

I'm not hungry

A: I wanted to make something nice

B: Okay

A: .

B: .

A: Are you going on any holidays this year.

B: Sorry

A: Are you having a holiday

B: I don't know

A: Okay

B: Okay.

A: .

B: .

A: You work hard, you should have a holiday

B: Okay.

A: You could go somewhere warm

B: Right

A: With a beach

B: Yes

A: You liked that when you were little

B: Right

A: You could take the baby

B: Obviously

A: .

   Sorry

B: Obviously if I go anywhere I'll take the baby

A: Yes

B: Yes

A: .

B: .

A: .

   Okay.

B: .

A: .

B: What are you basing that on

A: Sorry

B: That I liked beaches – what are you basing that on?

A: .

   I took you to beaches

B: When did that happen?

A: .

   I took you to a beach

B: Right

A: I have a photo

B: No

A: Of you on a beach

B: I don't think so

A: I had it on my wall

B: You didn't

A: You're wearing this blue hat and nothing else and you're
   really smiling

B: No

A: Yes

B: Not me

A: I had it on my wall

B: You possibly had a picture of A baby in a blue hat really
   smiling on your wall but that wasn't me.

   .

A: Okay

B: Okay

A: .

   It's funny.

   .

   That's funny – that thing we both do

B: .

A: That thing we both do where we both say Okay all the
   time.

   That's funny.

   That's nice.

   .

B: I have to go

A: Okay.

. 

okay.

Okay okay.

B: I've got work in the morning

A: Okay

B: I have to get up early

A: Okay

B: My back is killing – I'm up peeing about three times a night

A: Of course.

Okay.

B: .

Thank you for the pasta

A: You're welcome

B: Thank you for boiling some water and sticking a bag of pasta and three kilos of salt in it.

A: .

. 

That's okay.

I'm sorry.

B: For what.

A: I'm sorry you didn't like it

B: Didn't like what

A: The pasta

B: That's fine. For that, you have my full and total forgiveness.

A: Thank you.

.

I'll do something better next time.

B: .

A: .

.

It's raining.

It's been raining a lot.

Quite like it.

Nice. Soothing.

You liked it when you were little.

The rain.

I have this picture of you in your wellies

B: Okay

A: In some puddles

B: Alright

A: And you're really smiling

B: Nope

A: And

B: Nope

A: You're clapping your hands together

B: Not me

A: It's really lovely

It's a Really beautiful photo.

.

.

.

It was my favourite thing.

To look at.

Inside.

.

Thank you for coming.

B: .

A: Next time I'll make something better.

Nut roast.

Kale super smoothies.

Avocado on.

On Rice cakes.

Or

B: I say Okay because I literally haven't got any other words to say to you.

A: .

that's okay.

B: I say Okay because I cannot summon Any other words when I am in your company.

A: .

B: I say Okay because when I look at you my mind goes completely blank and it is like my whole existence prior to these moments has been ebbed away and like I cannot imagine anything in the future even though I am a walking fucking embodiment of Futures and potentials and hopes because of what I am full of, which is what it Ought to have been for you. With me. Except it wasn't.

Except you were Shit at it.

Except you couldn't do it.

Except you Just Were Not There – you have not been in my life.

And that's fine. That's Okay – I have made my peace with that because it was Necessary and because I don't think it was entirely your fault, but now I can't Construct a relationship with you because you've decided to get your shit together thirty years too late.

I say Okay to fill a silence because I can't Bear it when you do.

.

.

A: I drew you.

I drew pictures of you. In hats and wellies and cooking and smiling.

I'm sorry.

.

B: That doesn't mean it fucking happened.

　　.

A: No.

　　No it doesn't.

　　No it didn't.

　　.

　　*B leaves.*

　　.

　　okay.

## 60. VICTORIA SPONGE.

**This scene is between two adults (A and B).**

A: Hello

B: .

A: Hi.

B: .

A: Yeah

B: Where's NAME1

A: At home.

　　.

　　With his Dad

　　.

　　Yeah

B: Right

A: Yeah

B: Right

A: Some

Playstation game or X Box or Nintendo or.

Thing on. On.

B: Gosh. All three consoles. My kids fight to play Snake on my old Nokia.

.

I'm kidding.

I'm making a joke from my tiny council house.

A: Right. Sorry. Yes.

B: Yes my house is tiny?

A: Not yes, I'm not.

I didn't Say.

I'm not Trying to.

You said.

.

I'm sorry.

.

I.

Can I come in

B: Now?

A: Well

B: This minute

A: Yes.

.

Yes if I

If it's not too much

I mean.

Yes

B: It's not the best time.

A: I made a cake

B: .

A: A Victoria sponge

B: Well done you.

A: .

I didn't know what you liked

B: Well I wasn't allowed to come to your Coffee mornings so we probably missed out on the Our Favourite Cakes chat.

.

A: Everyone likes Victoria Sponge

B: I'm lactose intolerant.

.

A: I

B: I'm not.

I just don't want your cake.

A: .

B: I'm not really sure what it is you want

A: Might be easier to explain inside

B: There's not really any room.

.

It really is Terribly small.

I'm not sure you and your cake would fit inside.

.

May as well say what you need to say right here.

.

A: Okay.

.

I'm sure you've heard – .

.

B: .

A: This is really hard for me to.

.

Of course you've heard, everyone's heard.

I'm in court next week.

B: Goodness. I had no idea.

A: Right

B: What a shock

A: And I'm not expecting to come home immediately.

Obviously we, I, hope that isn't the

But.

I've been told to prepare myself for the worst.

B: And the worst is

A: .

Some time away

B: Away

A: Yes

B: Spa break or

A: No

B: Cotswolds or

A: That's not

B: Caribbean perhaps

A: In prison.

.

B: I see

A: Yes

B: Right

In prison

A: Yes

B: Gosh

A: Yep

B: And this is my business, how exactly?

A: .

B: .

A: My kids.

My children are very fond of your children.

B: How nice.

A: Our children are friends

B: My children have lots of friends

A: Yes

B: Yes?

A: Yes, I'm sure your children have lots of friends

B: Is that a judgement

A: No

B: Are you Judging my kids

A: What

B: Lots of friends – you think they're feral or

A: Obviously that's not what I said

B: But you Think it

A: This is ridiculous

B: Now I'm being ridiculous

A: I didn't Say that

B: No, but you're thinking it

A: Isn't this exhausting for you?

B: You don't let my kids in your house.

A: .

    That's not true.

B: Well, it is. I mean. We both know it is. So. I don't know for whose benefit you're lying.

A: .

B: You won't let my kids step foot on your carpet. Or wood stripped floors or marble shitting hallways or whatever floor arrangements you've got going on over there – you won't let them play on All the Consoles or with the latest Lego or with the dogs or stay for the organic home cooked meals and play in the Massive treehouse out back. I know about the Massive

    Treehouse because Your kids sneak My kids in there sometimes.

A: .

    I haven't been kind enough. Certainly. I'm very sorry.

    My children are Fond of your children -

B: And My Kids Love your kids. They Love them Fiercely.

    They don't Do fond. They aren't fucking fifty.

    And I Love your kids. They're Funny. They're Cheeky. They're brilliant, kind, sweet kids.

    .

    Why are you here?

A: I

B: Is it because you think I can give you a run down of what prison might be like?

A: No.

B: Because I can't.

A: I don't. I didn't. That's not why I'm here.

B: .

A: My children haven't done anything wrong.

My children could really use some support and friendship.

And Love. Some of that Love. Fiercely.

I'm not asking for me.

I'm not Asking for me.

## 61. APPLICATION.

**This scene is between two adults (A and B).**

A: Your application has been accepted.

B: .

What?

A: The Board has reviewed your application, and you've been awarded a place.

B: Are you

A: Yep

B: Oh

A: Congratulations

B: Oh

A: You've worked very hard.

B: Fuck.

Sorry.

A: Would you like a biscuit?

B: No.

Thank you.

A: Feeling nauseous?

B: No actually. No. I've. No, it's all been really straightforward. I'm.

Thank you.

It's all been really.

Fine.

So far.

I'm incredibly lucky.

I'm very very very lucky.

Thank you.

A: You must be feeling pleased.

B: .

Yes.

A: Relieved?

B: Yes.

Yes.

Yeah.

Course.

Yes.

Yes.

I'm.

Sorry.

They told me it probably wouldn't happen.

A: No

B: They told me to prepare myself for the worst.

A: Well.

The places are limited and you've worked very hard.

The Board were impressed with your progress.

B: .

Right.

Thank you.

A: She.

It is a girl you're having?

B: No.

I mean.

I don't know.

I didn't want to find out.

I sort of assumed none of this would happen.

.

I've been trying to.

Look after it

and

just.

Assumed I wouldn't.

.

I'm sorry.

A: It's a shock.

B: .

A: Well.

Baby will be with you for a maximum of 18 months after birth.

But. The length of your sentence means that we're working towards your release date coinciding with it being Baby's time to go too.

B: Right.

.

So. I'll be moving.

A: Yes.

B: Right.

A: Absolutely.

There are ten places on the Mother and Baby Unit.

Just Ten.

That's a really incredible thing you've achieved.

B: .

It takes my kids about two hours to get here at the
moment.

.

And this. This is

Even Further.

A: .

B: So.

That's.

I'm just.

That's just something I'm.

Thinking about.

Because.

I'm not sure they.

.

I'm sorry.

I didn't think this would.

I'm sorry.

They have never felt Chosen.

So.

By me.

I think.

They will feel.

Find this Hard.

Think that I've perhaps.

Chosen Not Them.

Again.

And I'm.

I.

.

I thought.

If I Applied then I'm doing my best by This baby.

But that

I wouldn't get in.

And then nothing would be different for my other ones.

The ones at.

At.

Home.

So I'm just.

I'm just Processing what that.

What I can Do about.

About that.

.

A: This is something that was discussed when you Applied

B: Yes

A: So it's not an entirely new thought

B: No

A: You're not thinking of turning it down

B: .

A: If you Do turn it down, your baby will be taken into care.

B: .

A: Your current children are with your sister, is that right

B: Yes

A: And would she take the baby

B: I don't.

.

    She's very angry with me.

.

A: This is an opportunity for you to Bond with this baby

B: Yes

A: You know how precious those first months are

B: Yes

A: How Vital they are

B: They're All vital though.

    Aren't they?

    All the days, weeks, months – they're All vital. There are no recommended ones to miss.

.

    I just.

    I.

no.

## 62. SEVEN 2.

**This scene is for one adult (A).**

*A phone rings. A runs to pick it up.*

A: Hello?

Hello sweetheart –

Nothing, I picked up as quick as I

Seven rings? Are you sure?

.

Okay. Okay my love. I'll be quicker.

I'm fine.

Yes, I'm fine.

Yes.

I'm in a garden.

It's a garden centre. I'm having a cup of coffee.

I'll be leaving soon.

I'll be home by 2.

2.30.

Just some other customers. A lady who works here.

No, no I'm not.

Yes.

I talked to NAME.

About half an hour ago.

Just about how she was, how things are going.

Not much, just said she was a bit tired.

That she was looking forward to going away for a while.

She asked about you.

I said you were working hard but well. Top sets.

That was it.

I'm sure.

Yes.

Yes.

*Checks her pocket.*

Yep. Right here.

*Lifts the keys out of her pocket and jangles them near the phone.*

I had a salad. And a cake.

Yes.

Yes.

No.

No alcohol.

.

Yes.

All of it.

Properly.

I have a coat on.

I've got my hat.

Yes.

Of course.

2.30.

Yes.

.

I won't.

I will.

Every time.

I'll be at home.

Yes.

Yes, I'll wait by the window.

If you like.

I won't answer unless it's you.

.

Yes. I paid them.

All of them.

Okay.

Okay.

Okay.

Ten minutes? Okay. Yes. It's on vibrate. And loud. I'll pick up quicker.

I love you.

I love you.

I love you.

I love you.

I love you.

I love you.

Okay, sweetheart.

It's okay.

It's okay.

It's okay.

It's okay.

I can stay on the phone, it's okay.

NAME.

It's okay.

## 63. ICE.

**This scene is for four adults (A, B, C and D).**

A: Sorry sorry

B: Don't

A: We were caught in

B: Don't even

C: Really / sorry

D: Come on it's

A: Caught in

D: Please

A: / Traffic

C: / The weather was

B: Ahhhhh

D: See

C: Traffic – Traffic, we were / caught in

B: / You said weather

D: You very clearly said weather

C: The weather And the traffic

A: You're such a

C: The Weather was

B: Oh my God weather is Such a / Shit Excuse

D: / The Worst Excuse – who the fuck says they're late 'cos
   of The Weather when we can all look outside and see that
   the weather is – in fact – entirely fucking normal

C: This Heat is not normal – This Heat has been the cause of

B: Don't lie, you're such a Horrible liar

D: Mmmm

B: I really Like you, don't Lie and make me Hate you I Hate
   Liars you Know this

D: Didn't get your story straight

B: Rookie mistake

D: You were shagging, presumably

B: Or fighting, more likely – look at their / faces

D: / Those little faces

261

A: We brought wine

B: You're sweet – on the table

C: Two colours

D: Your generosity won't make us change the subject you
   fuckers

B: You're all red

D: Don't be embarrassed

B: It's such a lovely thing you like each other enough to still
   Fight

D: Or shag

B: Anyone can shag – if you're fighting you still Care – good
   for you guys

D: And it's even lovelier that you're so bad at lying

B: So bad

A: I'm sorry, can I sit down I feel like I might fall over.


B: Oh my God are you alright

D: Jesus, course you can

B: Fuck

D: Your face just

B: You look wiped out – are you okay

D: We were winding you Up I didn't realise you

B: You should have said something

A: My knees just

B: Here, have some water

A: Gave way, I didn't

B: It's okay

A: Just had a bit of a

C: We had a shock

D: Right

A: No

C: On the way here

D: Okay

A: No

D: Are you

B: What kind of shock

A: .

C: We

A: Don't.

   .

   Sorry.

B: Are you

A: It's just.

   Sorry.

   We.

   Sorry.

   Fuck.

Can I have some more water please.

D: .

Of course.

B: What's going on

A: We said we wouldn't

C: I know, but you

A: I'm fine

C: You don't Look fine

D: Is everything okay

A: Have you got any vodka

B: I

D: Yes

B: Is that

A: Can I have a massive glass of vodka please.

.

A Massive one please. With ice. With Cubes of ice, not crushed I know your fridge does crushed ice and I know that's very Impressive but I'd like ice I'd like it Cubed.

D: .

Um.

.

Okay.

C: I don't think

B: I'm sorry – what is

A: Can I just have a drink first.

.

.

C: We saw something

A: Shut up

C: We saw something

A: Could you shut up please

C: We Saw some/thing

A: / ShutthefuckingfuckupfuckfuckUp Now please

D: Um

B: Sorry – I'm a bit uncomfortable with -

C: We said we wouldn't say anything. We said we were just going to keep it between ourselves – that is why she is telling me to Shut Up, but I think things are different now that you are about to pass out on their kitchen floor

A: I'm not about to Pass Out

D: Do you guys need some time alone or

B: We were just Joking. About the fight

D: The shag

B: Shut up

A: It's like when you've been drinking and you move Location – you go outside for a fag and you're suddenly like Shit. I am Really Properly Pissed – and the world goes a bit off balance

D: Okay

A: D'you know what I mean though

D: Did you get fucked before you came here or

C: No

D: 'Cos that's a little fucking rude

C: Obviously we didn't Do that she's

A: But d'you know what I mean

B: I mean, I have a cassoulet in the oven and I think we just
     thought we were going to have dinner and now you're

A: Okay

B: I mean, I made fucking soda bread

C: There's a man covered in blood outside your house.

B: .

D: Pardon.

C: On the pavement, there's a man covered in blood.

D: Are you

A: Was.

D: Sorry

A: He's making it sound like There Is – there Was a man

B: I'm

C: Yes yes yes he got Up

B: I don't

A: So you decided to tell them then

C: He got up and ran off

B: I don't

C: He was covered in blood – there was loads of it

A: You're exaggerating – he's exaggerating

C: He was Swaying. Properly Staggering around.

D: Are you

B: Sorry, is this

A: Can I have some more vodka

B: No

A: If I help myself, can I just have some more vodka

B: I said no

A: .

Will you stop me though?

*Grins.*

If I just.

Walk over to the bottle.

Pick it Up.

And pour myself a glass.

Are you going to Do anything to stop that from happening – stop me following through on that?

.

C: We didn't See anything else

A: That's true

C: We just saw this man covered in blood

A: With a bit of blood – this is Very Good Vodka

C: Get up from a lying down position

A: He was crouched – he was Sitting, he wasn't Lying

C: And then sort of Stagger off towards that Alleyway

B: What Alleyway

C: That's not – that doesn't seem like the important piece of

A: And I'm not getting involved

B: Excuse me?

A: I didn't want to say anything because I'm not getting involved.

D: .

C: .

B: Sorry, I can't quite tell what you're

A: We couldn't Do anything

C: We asked if he was okay – I Asked him if he was okay, I said 'scuse me, are you okay

A: That's true – he did – it was Exactly like that

C: And he sort of Lurched

A: You're using really Hyperbolic language

C: Hyperbolic?

A: Really exaggerating for sort of Poetic effect

D: Is this a

C: I'm not trying to be Poetic

A: And then he just Ran off

C: I'm not writing fucking Poetry

B: Sorry, can you be

D: Our kids are upstairs

A: Milo and Mavis

B: That's not her name that's not their names

D: Can you not take the piss out of my kid's name

B: Every Single Time

A: I mean they might as well be called that

D: There was a knife on the street

B: A Knife is on our street

A: You own the whole street now?!

B: Sorry – can you just be Serious for

A: Our – you said Our street

B: Yes, collectively – Our – I feel part of a community – I'm
    sorry, I don't really follow your

A: There's no CCTV on that bit of road

D: Okay?

    .

A: I checked.

B: That's weird. That is a Weird thing to do

D: Your wife is fucking nuts. Okay? Your Wife has fucking
    Lost the plot

C: That's

D: I mean – Lovably so – I'm saying that With Love

B: I'm not

A: I'm not doing it – I'm not Getting Involved in something like – I have kids and I've Seen what this kind of thing Is

.

Not doing it.

Not doing it! Not doing it not doing it – It can Fuck right off.

.

Cheers.

.

B: I'm sorry – can I just. Can I.

Can I just

Clarify

Because I.

.

Are you saying you walked past a man who had just been fucking Stabbed outside our house and are you saying that you walked past because you have Kids and because you don't fancy the Hassle of Helping – are you saying that you Saw a Bleeding Man and the Thought that went through your head was about how it Might Impact your evening, not not Concern for him or – are you Laughing – are you fucking Laughing at

A: I'm just. No. Sorry. Yes. I Am laughing, yes I am laughing at you.

D: Are you guys having some problems? Because this is.

A: It's just.

Who do you think can Hear you?

.

B: Excuse me?

A: For whose benefit was all that fucking Rubbish you just Splattered out of your Stupid Stupid Fat Red mouth?

B: .

D: Okay now

A: No one can Hear you no one here thinks you're Actually That person who gives a shit about the Kind of person we just saw covered in blood outside your house

C: You said covered in blood was an exaggeration

A: The vodka's warmed me up – I don't Know what kind of image you've conjured up in your head of the scene that we're describing 'B' but it wasn't some Kid who lives on this street bleeding to death in your exceptionally clean gutters

C: Bleeding to Death

D: And how the fuck would you know that

A: .

D: How would You know that this Kid didn't live on this street?

A: .

I feel like you're Trying to make me laugh now

D: What are you On

B: just / leave it 'D'

A: / How did I Know that? How did I Know this kid was not Your people Your neighbour – how could I possibly have / come to that conclusion

D: / Yeah – Yeah – That's what I'm asking / you

A: That he's not the Dentist's son or the Lawyers son or the Charming adopted child from the house in the Mews at the / end of the road

C: / I think you need to / calm down

A: / Well I didn't ask him what his postcode was 'D' if that's what you're / getting at

D: / Then I don't know how you Know that

A: Because he looked Dirt Fucking Poor.

Because he could not have looked Less like he belonged in Your Gutters.

Because if we'd Hauled him in here

And Laid him out on your cream rugs

and Watched you Try not to notice his blood splattering up onto your white white walls

You Might have thought

Oh Fuck. How do we help this poor kid.

But you first thought would have been Disgust.

And Who the Fuck is he. And what's he doing in my Home. Whilst my children Sleep.

And I'm not fucking Judging that – I'm not saying your reaction should be anything Other than that – I'm Empathising, I'm Relating I'm Identifying okay good words right – I'm just saying that we should all be fucking

272

Honest about the fact that getting involved in that kind of shit – that kind of shit that happens All The Time to people Nothing like us – is no good is bullshit is nothing I'm interested in.

I give to charity.

I pay more than my fair fucking share of tax.

We're not people who get our hands fucking dirty.

And I'm just being Honest about that.

Is what I'm saying.

Is what I'm fucking saying.

.

B: Did you say Kid?

A: .

Sure.

I don't know.

What would you say?

C: .

16?

*A makes a noise.*

15?

14 maybe, maybe a Small 14 year old.

.

B: You could've called an ambulance.

A: .

Yeah.

I could've.

.

I didn't though.

.

He got up.

.

He moved out of my eyeline.

.

Done.

## 64. BATH.

**This scene is between two adults (A and B).**

A: I just saw the strangest thing.

B: Hi

A: Sorry.

I did though.

B: Okay

A: .

How was your day?

B: D'you want to talk about it

A: No I want to hear / about your day

B: / This Strange Thing

A No I. No. Don't do [that].

Sorry.

Where are the kids

B: Upstairs

A: Are they

B: Sleeping

A: Sorry

B: What happened

A: I don't

B: D'you want something to eat

A: No

B: Why don't you just tell me what happened

A: No it's

B: You Clearly Want to

A: No I'm

B: Fine

A: No.

Fuck.

Bread. Have we got bread?

B: Loads.

I'm going upstairs.

I want to read a book.

Have a bath.

Glass of wine.

Bottle of wine.

A: There was this girl

B: .

Okay

A: She was stood outside the chippy

B: Right

A: Glass everywhere

B: .

A: Like – fucking Everywhere

B: Okay

A: Police

B: Right

A: I had to

B: What

A: I had to make a statement

B: What about

A: Give my number and

B: Right

A: I feel really sick

B: Have some water

A: I can't, I feel like I'll

B: Sorry

A: Feel like I'll vomit

B: I'm sorry

A: Why're you Sorry

B: I was pissed off you were late

A: I know

B: I didn't ask you about – I'm sorry

A: I was late because I had to give a statement

B: Yes

A: I had to give them my number

B: Okay

A: I'm sorry I was late

B: No – Jesus, no, I'm sorry, I'm really sorry for not being Kind.

A: Not being kind in general or now?

B: .

Are you serious?

You want to do that Now? I – .

.

I am Allowed to be Pissed off you were late you are Regularly Fucking Late I.

.

You've had a shock.

A: Can I go and see them

B: Who

A: The kids, can I go and look at them

B: They only just went

A: I want to see that they're asleep

B: Becomes a bit pointless if you wake them up

A: I won't wake them

B: You will

A: I'll be quiet

B: I'm with them All the time, you'll Definitely wake them if
   you go up you are Incapable of being Fucking Quiet your
   fucking Shoes and your fucking Breathing and your.

   .

   Sorry.

   I'm sorry. I'm not trying to.

A: She had blood

   All over her wrists

B: Jesus

A: She looked so small

B: It's okay

A: She had bits of glass and blood in her hair

B: It's okay

A: And a bat

B: A bat

A: Yeah, a bat – this

   Bat

B: What happened

A: She wasn't crying

B: No

A: She just looked so small and so tired and so fragile and little and

B: It's okay

A: Why d'you keep saying it's okay

B: Because you're upset

A: But it's not okay

B: But you're okay

A: Yes

B: And the kids are okay

A: Yes

B: And you've had a shock

A: Yes

B: And we'll be okay

A: Will we?

B: Are you trying to tell me something?

A: No.

B: Are you Trying to start a different kind of conversation Right Now

A: No

B: It Feels like you are

A: Stop fucking Making it about you this is Palpably Not about You Jesus Christ.

I'm sorry.

She won't be. She won't be okay.

.

B: She might be.

A: She won't. She was Absolutely Furious. She completely
Lost it. She needs Help

B: She'll get help

A: From?

B: .

Police

A: Oh right.

B: Services

A: Services?

B: I don't know – yeah – services

A: Excellent. That's all okay then.

.

B: Why are you being so Awful to me?

A: I'm Not I'm Fucking Upset

B: Well I'm sorry about that but I don't know what you Want
me to say

A: I want you to stop Lying

B: Lying

A: And saying it will All Be Okay

B: Fine it'll all be Shit it'll all be absolutely Shit and she'll get no help and she won't be okay is that better is that the is that what you.

Fuck this shit. Wine and a bath I just wanted Wine and a Bath

.

A: I've seen her before.

B: .

Who

A: This girl, I've seen her before

B: Right

A: I didn't say that to the police, should I have

B: Well they've got your number

A: I think I wrote it down wrong

B: I'm sure you didn't

A: I've seen her walking around before. Pissed. Crying. Alone.

B: .

Who is she

A: Just a girl. Just some Little girl. Always caked in make up. Wearing heels she can't walk in. Ladders in her tights. Birds nest hair. I've seen her falling over. And not done anything. I've just watched her.

.

She's about the same age as -

Where are the kids?

It's warm in here.

It's really warm.

## 65. LETTER.

**This scene is between two adults (A and B).**

A: Fuck you.

B: That's.

   .

Okay.

Okay.

Let's start again shall we.

Hi.

A: Fuck you harder.

B: Why don't you have a seat

A: Are you taking the piss

B: .

No. No, I'm not.

*A cries. For a long time.*

B: Okay.

   .

Alright.

   .

Okay.

.

Why don't you tell me what's going on

A: You Know what's going on

B: I don't

A: You said you'd help me

B: I'd be delighted to help you if I can.

.

A: You don't remember me, do you?

B: .

Yes.

A: Jesus Christ

B: Look

A: This is fucking

B: Okay

A: Outrageous

B: .

A: Outrageous is the fucking word – I've never had fucking
Cause to say the word before but Fuck Me this is
Outrageous

B: Look, I'm

A: Busy – yes yes yes yes yes yes yes I know you're busy – I
know its on its fucking knees, but

B: .

A: I haven't been able to stop crying.

B: Okay.

A: It's not okay though, is it.

.

You looked at the inside of my vagina.

Maybe it'd jog your memory on who the hell I am to take another look at the inside of my vagina

B: Look

A: You see a lot of vaginas

B: Okay

A: No

B: Okay

A: Nope.

B: .

You're upset.

A: Yes.

You took swabs.

B: .

A: It hurt.

B: .

A: You measured the length of a bruise on my thigh.

B: .

A: You stitched up my forehead

B: .

A: You said that wasn't what you normally did but I was getting blood on your carpet.

B: .

A: You said it in a nice way.

B: .

A: You said it in a way that made me feel about five years old in a good way in a way that made me feel Held in a way I Don't get to feel I don't get to feel Held

B: .

A: I Sobbed.

I Sobbed and you held my head and you kissed the top of it.

B: Well I don't. I don't think I.

Right

Look.

Yes, I remember.

A: You Do remember

B: Of course I remember

A: Cos you didn't about two minutes

B: Of Course I remember

A: You weren't so sure a second ago

B: I remember you very vividly, I remembered you a second ago two minutes ago I remember you I remember you I was I was struggling remembering that I had behaved. I had behaved

A: You had behaved

B: I had behaved

A: You had behaved

B: Unprofessionally.

.

A: .

You were Kind to me.

Profess[ional] – you were Kind / to me

B: / You really ought to have an appointment

A: You told me to get out

B: I

A: Of the relationship – You told me I should leave him

B: I don't think I

A: You told me I was putting my kids at risk

B: I'm not sure I Phrased it in that

A: You put me onto Legal Aid

B: Okay

A: As an Idea

B: Look

A: As in, they didn't Exist for me and you Told me about them and Essentially Invented the Concept of Tangible Help

B: Invented is

A: Yes you Fucking Did

B: I

A: You wrote down websites – I stuck them to my fridge

B: I don't think I was quite so Strong or or or

As Vocal as

A: And then you send me a letter telling me that my doctors
letter – my doctors letter that I need From you in order to
qualify for any fucking legal aid in order to prove that my
husband beat the shit out of me – was going to cost me
seventy quid.

.

B: Well.

That's.

Yes.

That's how these.

Yes.

.

A: How much are you getting paid

B: Okay

A: Are you not getting enough money

B: Look

A: Are you strapped for cash

B: That's not

A: Cos I thought you were paid Reasonably well.

Considering.

I mean I know you're here all the fucking time and it's
awful yada yada yada but

.

I clean. I literally clean shit off of porcelain.

Shall we Compare Bank Balances?

.

B: That's not

A: And that day. That day he stamped on my face and kicked
my vagina in – That day wasn't even the worst day, not
by a longshot okay not by a long shot and I thought you
Got that okay – it took quite a lot to come in here and
bleed on your floor and have you hold my head like my
mother should have like the Idea of a mother Would have
like the perfect perfect idea of a Mother Does and tell me
everything might be okay, that there might be this thing
called Hope for me, this thing called Hope that I had just
assumed wasn't really For me – you made that Exist, you
Birthed that and Gifted it to me and I appreciate that That
is a lot for you to Comprehend to wrap your brain around
but You Did That, so to get your letter telling me I had to
Pay for that help actually, that I needed to give you Cash
to legitimise that fairly fundamental experience of what I
had thought was basic, human Care, to get the equivalent
of you not stroking my head but Caving it fucking in
with a Metaphorical Fucking Baseball Bat, was a bit of a
fucking shock.

Actually.

*B is crying.*

*A stares.*

B: .

We are having.

I am having a bit of.

At home.

There is.

Some.

Financials and.

But.

You're.

It was.

Thoughtless – I was.

Without thought.

But there is.

.

I remember you.

Of course I remember you.

I think about you often.

You were shaking. The whole time. You Shook. The entire time. I couldn't stitch your head up for ages because you were

Humming.

You were terribly brave.

And the blood.

It kept dripping.

And you barely noticed.

And I knew. Of course I knew that this was not

That this was not.

That this was not.

That this was not.

That this was not the. The. The. Worst time or the.

First or the.

Last or the.

My Mother.

Was.

.

That's not.

.

That's not.

.

Your concern that's.

.

If you can just sit there. For a minute. For one.

For.

Then I can.

If you can just hang on a.

Just.

Then.

Then I'll just write this up.

I'm.

I'm very.

.

.

*B Types out a letter. This should take as long as it takes. Prints it. Hands it over.*

*A Leaves.*

## 66. TRANSFERENCE.

### This scene is between two adults (A and B).

A: Can I make you a cup of tea?

B: .

A: Or a glass of water – can I get you a glass of water

B: This is my house

A: Yes exactly, can I get you something to drink

B: Excuse me

A: Or can I call someone for you

B: What are you

A: Is there anyone I can call for you

B: I live here

A: Yes

B: You don't live here

A: No I don't

B: So I

A: I live about fifteen miles from here

B: I'm sorry

A: You're sorry for where I live

B: No, I'm not Apologising that wasn't an apology it was a a a

A: Confusion – it was about you feeling Confused

B: About why you're telling me where you live exactly

A: I live near the marshes

B: I don't give a fuck I was expressing General confusion I'm feeling Generally Confused about what it is you think you're doing

A: Right

B: Offering me tea and

A: Right

B: Water and

A: Yes

B: Giving me your fucking postcode when I've not asked for it

A: I didn't give you my postcode

B: .

    I Know you didn't that was

A: Yes

B: Sarcasm or

A: Yes

B: Disbelief or

A: Yes

B: I'm having an Out of Body experience

A: Yes fine

B: I don't want you to be here

A: No

B: I want you to Get the Fuck Out

A: Okay

B: Okay as in you Will get the Fuck Out

A: I'm going to ask you to stop swearing at me

B: You're going to as in you're About to or you're going to as in you're in / the process of

A: / No no I'm in the the Process of – exactly

B: Right

A: Thank you

B: Right

A: Right

B: Okay

A: I'm nervous

B: .

A: I'm very nervous – I shouldn't be saying that

B: No

A: I shouldn't be telling you that

B: No

A: Because I imagine that You're feeling pretty nervous

B: Do you

A: Yes, yes I imagine that My presence, My being here is causing You to feel some apprehension and Nerves and that that

B: Right

A: In turn is causing Me to feel Nervous

B: I

A: And I'm sure that me now Talking about feeling nervous is Increasing any anxiety that You might be feeling

B: Look

A: Transference or

B: What

A: My Mother – my Mother worked as a Psychiatric Nurse for fifteen years she would say words like Transference to me and I think that's what

B: You're using that word incorrectly

A: Okay

B: Your Mother would tell you that you are using that word incorrectly

A: Okay

B: But you're right that You standing in my living room talking about Your nerves is not helping my own state right now and I assume that you are here that you have been Dispatched here

A: Dispatched is a

B: In order to

A: Good word

B: In order to Help Me in some way but it has Somehow
become all about you and I assume you are here to tell
me that something awful has happened that something
completely irreversible has happened and that actually
you are supposed to do that and offer Some kind of
support or

A: Your daughter is dead.

.


.


I'm so sorry.

That came out very badly I really apologise.

That wasn't.

That wasn't what.

I Practised.

That's not. Again – I shouldn't say that – that's not.

But I did.

Whole way here – in the car – in the Car – I practised
over and over – what words and How and. Of course,
when you practise that sort of thing – this sort of thing –
this kind of scenario – the thing you end up doing – and
particularly as the journey is not a short journey – I I I I
I ended up hearing your responses and I confess I started
with the Offer of of Tea and Water and In my head how
it played out in my head You – the Fabricated Version of
You that I was talking to, who was taller Incidentally, than
you are – In My Head this is, whilst I was driving – well

295

She – You that is – Accepted the Tea and then I had time – in the Version in my Head – I had time to Compose myself and look around at your walls and your floors and your ceiling and then perhaps make an assessment on How best to to phrase it – what I Mean is that the kettle boiling time would have allowed Me the time to Really Rehearse what I was planning on Saying, to really Go Over the Words I was going to use to tell you about your daughter's death and to to to Construct that sentence with Though And Care that sentence that I knew might make your Knees Buckle – that's the phrase, that's the phrase that my Colleagues said to Describe but it's it's – but anyway – and So the – because I knew, I do profoundly Understand that the Semantics of that, that you might really form Memories Based on my Choice of words – my Uncle died in a rowing accident when I was seventeen and often when I think of his life and certainly his death I remember very clearly How that information was delivered to me – my Aunt was a a a Drinker so they were very Confused and I think I found that very Difficult very Complicated at the time and Undoubtedly my Nerves and anxiety around water and Boats more specifically – Small Boats to be precise – but this I this I I this I has Not been what I – that was all irrelevant and I.

I'm so sorry.

I'm so profoundly sorry.

.

We offer our deepest condolences.

.

B: You're very young.

A: Yes.

Thank you.

B: I thought they sent two.

A: That doesn't.

We've been experiencing.

.

Anymore.

.

B: I don't really drink tea.

A: .

Anything. Can I get you

Anything?

B: .

No.

Thank you.

.

Do you know what happened?

Do you know How she.

I'm assuming She.

Isn't that funny.

I mean.

It's not fucking cancer is it.

Do you.

do you.

I'm not Asking. I just want to know If you know.

A: *Nods.*

B: .

Can I see her?

A: *Nods.*

B: When I see her.

Will it be obvious.

How she [died].

Will it be obvious.

Will I know.

A: *Nods.*

B: When she was little, she was so happy.

I know everyone says that. I do.

But She.

She wasn't Easy. Huge Huge Emotions.

From Nowhere but.

She Was happy.

She Was.

And she won't get to be now. She won't get to be thought
of as Happy that can't be Anyone's abiding memory
of her because this last percentage has been so terribly
terribly terribly terribly Sad.

Was it her neck?

A: .

*Nods.*

B: .

Was she on her own for long?

A: .

I. I don't.

There will be an inquest.

.

B: You didn't know her.

A: I'm

B: They just Dispatch someone don't they.

Anyone.

It hadn't Dawned on me that you're telling my that my daughter killed herself and you probably don't even know what she looked like.

A: I'm sorry.

B: That's not your fault.

A: I'm sorry.

B: When you hang yourself you can lose consciousness quite quickly if you do it properly do you know if she did it properly?

With the

The

the

With the knot at the.

.

A: I'm so sorry.

B: If she did it properly then it won't have been a mistake.

It's That, I think, it's the idea that it's a.

If it was a Mistake then I'm not sure that I could.

.

Bear that and.

.

She was quite small. And she looked nothing like me. And her eyes were green.

A: I'm sorry.

B: I'm sorry about your uncle.

A: .

Thank you.

## 67. ENGLISH.

**This scene is for two adults (A and B).**

**The words in Bold are in another language to the language that is spoken in the rest of the scene – and the rest of the play. Any language.**

A: Okay. Okay okay okay – 'B'?

B: *Nods.*

A: Full name

B: 'B'

A: Okay

   Hand here

B: .

A: And the other hand

B: .

A: And look straight ahead

B:

A: Good. Okay. First time?

B: .

A: Sorry – first time Here? First time in This prison?

B: *Nods.*

A: How are you feeling?

B: .

   Okay.

A: .

   Here for theft?

B: .

A: You stole

   Right? You stole some stuff, yes?

   Some

   Nappies and

   the [fuck] are they [doing]

Anyway – okay – You Stole, yes?

B: .

*Nods.*

A: .

Ahhhh. Okay okay I right yeah I – You're pending
extradition. okay. that makes more [sense]

B: .

A: You speak English?

B: .

*Nods.*

Bit. A little.

A: Can you understand me? You're following everything I've
said so far?

B: .

A: .

I need you to Say yes if you / Do understand me

B: / Yes? Yes I

A: Yes – good

B: Yes

A: Good

B: Yes

A: Good. Okay. Good. No one told me – if you need a
translator

B: .

A: I can't do that right now, so if you need a translator

B: .

A: A translator

B: Translator

A: If You Need A Translator

B: .

*Nods*

A: You do?

B: *Nods*

A: But you understood that

B: .

*Nods*

A: You did

B: Yes

A: You understood me Ask if you need a translator

B: Yes

A: I mean. Translator. That's not a. That's not an Everyday Word that's not that's not Cat or Dog or

B: Dog

A: Translator is a more Obscure word than Dog

B: Dog

A: No I'm not saying dog

B: dog

A: No. No – I'm saying

B: Sorry

A: I'm saying Translator I'm

B: **I don't**

A: So – I'm just – I'm trying to figure out – because I've got a big old line there – I'm trying to Assess your Immediate needs – I'm trying to figure out if we can just do this bit – 'cos

B: I'm

A: So – we can get a translator to come down in a little while

In a Little While.

Okay?

B: .

*Nods.*

Okay.

A: .

You alright?

You okay?

B: *Nods.*

A: You've been in prison before

B: .

A: You. In Prison. Before.

B: *Nods.*

A: Can you talk me through your previous?

B: .

A: Always For Stealing?

B: .

A: Easier if you just say yes / sweetheart and then we can

B: / **I don't**

 **I don't know what you're**

A: You've been in prison before

B: *Nods.*

A: For stealing?

B: *Nods.*

A: Anything else?

B: .

A: Murder? Rape? Fraud?

B: **Murder?** murder? **Did you just. Are you fucking**

A: Joking we'll – okay

 D'you have family? Nearby?

B: **I'm sorry I don't / understand what**

A: / no no no no I don't understand / you can't

B: / **okay okay** okay Okay

A: I need you to speak English when you're talking to me
 okay

B: English

A: Exactly

B: Speak English

A: Perfect

B: Okay

A: There you go

B: Sorry?

A: So – Family? Girlfriend boyfriend? Mum? Dad? Near?
Here?

B: .

   Okay.

A: .

B: do I. **do I have a. You're asking about / my**

A: / Ah

B: My Mum. Yes. My. I have. / Mum.

A: / Okay great, good that's good

B: **My Mum can I Call my Mum –**

A: .

   We will get someone here for you – I just need to

B: I

A: I've got your date of birth as ten ten ninety eight?

B: .

A: Birthday?

B: Now?

A: fucking.

No. No – not. Your birthday

B: My birthday

A: Is the Tenth Of October

B: Ah

A: Nineteen Ninety Eight

B: Okay

A: Yes?

Here – look – these numbers – your birthday?

B: .

A: / Ijustneedyoutosay/yes – yes – good

B: / Yes – Yes

A: And this is your address?

B: .

A: This is where Mum is – where home is Where / You Live

B: / Yes? You

A: Presumably you're not registered with a GP, I'm going to /
   skip that

B: / what

A: Don't worry I'm / just

B: / I don't

A: Don't worry about it no one's registered with a GP it's

B: **I can't understand what you're**

A: we need to go through medical and I don't have a / clue
   how we're

B: / **I'm sorry I don't have a fucking clue what** / **you're**

A: / but we'll just – I mean – we can do this properly / once we've got a

B: / **I can't** I **look this is** can you / please

A: / translator but I can't – look okay okay okay

B: I'm

A: You can see a nurse in a bit

B: I

A: Any medical issues we need to know about?

B: .

A: You on any medication? Pills?

B: Drugs?

A: Legal ones – you on anything? Any conditions? Any problems? Have you got Any idea what I'm / talking about

B: / a nurse. yes please. a nurse

A: Yeah – you get to see the nurse next, but she doesn't speak. I. We need a translator.

B: Yes, a translator.

A: Are you ill?

B: .

A: In the head? Or body? Heart problems? Any self harm? Suicidal? Suicide? You know what that means, right? Are you likely to hurt yourself – kill yourself?

B: **Suicide? Do I know what it is or am I at Risk** / **of – I don't**

A: / Okay – any gangs we should know about? Any affiliation with. Jesus. i don't know why i'm – affiliations. As if you know what Affiliations means I

B: **I'm really scared. I'm really really scared**

A: Have you been involved in any Homophobic or Racist attacks or are you – do you Identify as I.

B: **I'm very sorry I broke the law. I really didn't mean to. I was just hungry. I wasn't thinking. I didn't think. I can be a bit Impulsive. I'm working on it. I just want to go home.**

A: .

    Okay.

B: **Do you understand me?**

A: .

B: **I'm very scared. I miss my mother. I'm scared I won't get out.**

A: I'm going to try and get you a translator. Okay?

B: **I get scared I won't wake up. I get scared that I won't get to see my Mum. Can I call her?**

A: .

    I don't understand what you're.

B: **Can I just get to hear her voice? Just for a bit.**

    **I'm really really really scared.**

A: I will try and get someone.

    You look frightened.

    Are you frightened?

B: .

*Nods.*

## 68. GARDEN.

**This scene is between two adults (A and B).**

*A garden centre. A buggy.*

A: Beautiful, isn't it?

B: .

Sorry?

A: The Magnolia.

B: Oh.

I didn't know its name.

A: .

When my girl was little, we didn't have a garden, I always used to sit her under this exact magnolia tree here in spring and she'd fall asleep.

B: Wow

A: Buggered for the rest of the year

B: Right.

A: She's twenty five now.

B: Gosh.

A: I know.

Happens before you know it.

B: .

I'll bet.

A: Such a cliche, isn't it.

'S'true though.

Cliche's are cliches for a reason.

She sleeps fine now.

Really Well in fact.

She's a Good sleeper.

B: .

It is beautiful.

.

A: Mmmm.

.

How old is she?

B: Six months.

A: Lovely.

Sleeping through yet?

B: .

No.

A: Hard.

Poor you.

She breastfed?

B: .

No.

A: No. Good for you.

Sorry. I don't mean. I just.

Either way. There's So much Pressure these days. God, my
nipples bled for Weeks. Insisted on keeping going though
– everyone told me that was best for baby, best for bloody
baby.

You think, I'm falling to pieces, my body is literally
Shredding, starting with the fucking nipples but This Is
Best For The Baby Is It?

God.

You start thinking about it and it Rushes back.

Sorry.

Found it Hard.

.

She's lovely.

B: Yes.

A: Very Alert, isn't she?

B: Yes.

A: Has she seen the ducklings?

They just hatched. Last week.

B: No. Not yet. Thought we'd sit in the sun a bit. Then go
round.

A: Lovely.

Lovely.

She your first?

B: .

    No.

    Yes.

    I mean.

    She's not mine.

A: .

    Oh.

    Sorry. I'm sorry – I assumed

B: I haven't got kids.

    Not yet

A: Right

B: One day

A: Lovely

B: That's what I [keep saying].

    But.

    .

    It [hasn't happened].

    .

    Yet.

    .

A: You here with those other women?

B: Yes

A: That's nice

B: Yes

A: Like a nanny group or

B: No.

    Not quite.

    Sort of.

    .

A: She'll be big enough for the swings soon

B: I think so

A: They're building some by the duck pond

B: I saw

A: They do Almond milk in the cafe now

B: Really

A: I volunteer here.

    I was a stay at home Mum for fifteen years. I've got five.
    Four really. Four now.

B: Oh I'm sorry.

A: I wanted to be a midwife.

    But I do love gardening.

    Mum one of those workaholics is she?

    My husband was.

    City types?

    Always thought that looked fun.

    Expect it's not.

Expect it's bloody hard work managing a career, a baby and childcare.

Poor thing.

Thank God she's got you.

B: No.

She's in prison.

A: .

Oh.

Right.

B: I work at the Mother and Baby Unit there.

A: I didn't know there was one

B: Prison?

A: No. God, you can't miss the prison. You can see it from my bedroom window.

It's quite a nice building.

From the outside.

Mother And Baby Unit.

Poor thing.

Sorry.

.

B: She likes this tree.

I think.

A: Yes.

I think so too.

What's her name?

B: I can't tell you that

A: No.

Right.

B: I shouldn't have said we were from the prison.

We come here every week.

I could get fired.

A: I won't.

I don't.

I can not say anything. If you like.

B: I'm not asking you that.

Obviously I can't ask you that so that's not what I'm asking.

A: No.

She is lovely.

B: Yes.

Very.

She's smiley.

A: Yes.

B: Out here.

Not so much in there

A: Oh

B: I don't think she smiles at her Mum I really don't.

A: It's very hard. It Must be

very hard. For all of you.

For everybody.

I think that most days. The world is a fucker for absolutely everybody really. In some way.

.

She's lovely.

B: Yes.

A: Not a sleeper.

B: No.

A: Doesn't want to miss anything.

B: No.

A: Lots to look at here.

B: Yes.

A: Fresh air and.

B: Yes.

A: Ducks and.

B: Yes.

A: Magnolia.

B: Yes.

A: Just for a couple of weeks.

B: Yes.

A: Joy for a couple of weeks isn't bad.

B: No.

A: Well. Well done you.

B: Yes. Yes.

A: It's Such a Beautiful day

B: Yes

A: My baby died.

B: .

A: It was Awful. She came out dead.

B: .

A: And Then – back Then – I'm very old now – Back Then
they used to take it off you straight away as though it
were a bit of cancer or tumour you'd Grown on Purpose
or through some Negligence or Lack of love or Ruined
bit of Womanly Equipment and they'd found it and you
were lucky they'd caught it in time but Oh God I've never
known pain like it.

Couldn't stand up straight for Weeks.

.

It doesn't go away.

.

It never goes away.

Even when the Heat of it is gone, the nub of it, the quick,
the pit, the belly or the middle – even when That is gone,
the memory of it is like putting a finger deep deep deep
in a wound and pushing that finger all the way down to its
knuckle and then scraping whatever bit of blood or flesh
or sinew or bone that you find there. With your nail.

I put her in a box and buried her under a tree in the garden.

B: A Magnolia tree?

A: No.

No.

B: Oh.

A: Yes.

An Apple tree. Could imagine her under an apple tree.

B: NAME1. Her name is NAME1.

## 69. BODIES.

**This scene is between two adults (A and B).**

*This is in a prison cell.*

A: I like women who Like their bodies.

I didn't realise this until her – I didn't Know that it
was specifically That that I liked, but it was and it is – I
think I thought I liked Confident women or or a kind of
Arrogance almost or maybe it was Happiness I thought I
was attracted to – like I wanted a happy, content sort of
woman – but I have realised – She made me realise – that

I like women who Like their bodies – not what they can
Do, not what their body is capable of Doing, but the body
Itself Not that Maternal Motherhood Shit, those Womanly
words about being a Home or a Vessel or a space for
something new, birthing or feeding, isn't it remarkable
that my body can sustain a human being, can keep
another human being alive – I'm not talking about that,
I'm not talking about a a a a Profound connection to the
earth, rooted through your biology – through your Tubes
and your Ovaries, the middle of you, through the milk
that comes and the liquids that burn not for you, but for
something unlatched and then refastened To you – I don't
mean that, I'm talking about selfishness and Those Words,
those roof of the mouth back of the teeth words were not
invented by women, that language has fuck all to do with
Womanhood, that kind of shit was invented by men – and
I have three kids okay so I'm not like Not Uninterested or
Uninvested or Notgivingashitaboutthe whole – it's just that
the Language of it all, the Language of bellies and babies
and ovaries and wombs and milk and milk and milk is
as though it is The Only language about our bodies that
we are allowed to be Euphoric about take Pride in great
lungfuls of Pride in as though we didn't all want to Walk
East and sleep in Fields and Talk to Truck Drivers and
fucking Construction Workers and Kings alike and and
look, I'm not you know, and Also, you know, you will
Need something to meditate on by the way, to obsess over
to gather and to knit to consume and to unspool, you will
find that One Fixed thing will help you here or you will
be fucking fucked – and Watching her Watching her and
Realising that she Liked Her Fucking Body was my one
activity my one fixation and now You are here, You are
here instead and I want to know whether you Like your
body against Walls or or floors or underneath windows or
against railings or bars or on a Bed on something Soft like
a mattress like a Good Mattress or or forget that actually,

320

a Hard mattress because I don't mean the object I don't
mean your body In Relation To the mattress, I mean your
Body because you Stand

You Lean

As though you fucking Hate it.

B: .

A: .

That soft bit of flesh. Near the bone by your shoulder.
When you press back against that wall and it curls under
on itself. When it gets hot up against something cool and
takes a moment to

Recalibrate

Adjust itself.

.

That wet bit.

Inside your mouth.

Like Mud.

.

That saliva. Needling down your throat. The fat above
your hip. The fat below your hip. The fat fat fat on your
thigh and your arm. Your cunt. Deep. And warm. Your
elbow – the inside of it, your ankle, blue black near the
bone.

.

You're like a little house. In the middle of a wood – dark,
pitch black, the air old and charcoal, not a bit of liquid,
not any star or sun or birdcall or moon, and you are the

house. Made of pine. In the middle of it. One light on.
One little bulb.

B: .

A: I want to catch you. I want to Feel

with my hands

with the bit of my hands, that vulnerable spot between
finger and thumb that when I fishhook it with my other
finger goes straight to my heart and makes me breathe in
all funny and little and cold like the bottom of a river cold
where it's sludge and slow – I want to catch you

beneath your arms

when you thought you might slip

and I want to

Sustain that feeling

of Just having caught you

And you Just having been caught

.

for as long as i possibly can.

### 70. DREAM.

**This scene is for two adults or two children or
one adult and one child (A and B).**

A: I had a dream last night.

B: .

A: [I know, I know].

.

It was about NAME1.

B: .

Oh.

.

A: I was being haunted. Violently haunted – a poltergeist

B: Exciting

A: Terrifying. Genuinely terrifying. Glasses, mirrors were
   smashed, rooms kept Flooding – not completely, but I'd
   walk in and look down and water would be trickling in
   from the corners, the edges of the room, only up to about
   the skirting board – do I mean skirting board?

B: .

[I don't know?]

A: Ankle deep

B: *Nods.*

A: Muddy. Not clear. Leaves sticking to my ankles. Head
   spinning. I was Terrified.

And then suddenly my Dad is there in front of me,
holding my face in his hands and he's shouting but I'm
still spinning – he sounds far away and then there's a
child next to me – Our child – and the child is shouting
'Mummy, look at Granddad' and I'm Looking and trying
to focus and He's saying – Dad, not the child – is saying,
it's okay it's okay it's okay it's okay it's Okay it's okay
and my head is so heavy I can barely keep it up but he's
Holding it and I say – Look, Look at all of this Water –
Look at All of this Water – and I Kick and it splashes and
they look at me like

323

What

the Fuck

are you On about and I realise, really slowly and really
Calmly with real Relief

that

oh God – there Is no ghost

B: Oh

A: There Is no no no

B: Poltergeist

A: Poltergeist exactly

B: what Is a poltergeist

A: like a a a Violent sort of

B: like with a / Vendetta

A: / ghost I – yes I suppose

B: right

A: like

B: Unfinished business

A: Yes I

B: right – sorry

A: And I realise that instead – Instead – what has happened is
that I am completely Mad

B: .

A: Insane – I've lost my Mind – and I'm Relieved, I'm
   relieved that there's no ghost, that ghosts continue to Not
   Be Real

B: yes

A: But there's a little Stone in my belly – at the top of my
   belly, the bottom of my chest there is a a Stone

B: a

A: because this means I'm mad.

   This means that I am mad again.

B: .

A: And then I'm Asleep – in the dream I'm asleep, and I
   wake up in a sort of um

   Cabin Bed?

   in a little hut on a beach somewhere really warm

B: because you sleep with a hot water bottle in June

A: and I climb down this ladder from my bed and there's a
   big table on the beach under this sort of canopy thing and
   there are lots of people eating breakfast, lovely holiday
   sort of breakfast, warm fresh bread and lots of fruit, sticky
   sort of peaches and strawberries and watermelon and I
   don't know anyone and then I spot NAME1 and I – oh
   my God – she's Alive – I can't – the Relief, I – tears
   rolling already and I sit down and everyone's talking,
   really lovely sort of quiet hum, and the sea must be
   nearby, must be right next to us 'cos I can hear water
   again and I can hear birds again and I sit and listen and I
   cannot take my eyes off her and she looks at me and she
   Smiles

   This

Smile and.

I just can't believe that she's Alive.

I tell her about the ghost – about the haunting. She tips her head to the side and smiles again, really warm, really kind, really really really fucking Sad – sad for me not for her – and she says, well, 'A', of course you felt like you were being haunted and I said.

how come.

that stone stuck in my throat.

and she says. well. because I Died, sweetheart.

.

and she.

.

she strokes my face. brushes back my hair. holds my chin.

.

And I look down. And my feet are wet. And her feet are wet. And. She Smiles the Biggest smile and opens her mouth to say something and.

.

And I wake up. Properly wake up – not just in my dream wake up. And my face is soaking. And I can still feel that stone in my throat.

And I wonder if it means that I'm supposed to follow her.

# 71. DOCUMENTARY.

**This scene could be for one adult (A) and the voice of
a second adult (B). Or B could be onstage also, perhaps
holding a camera – there should be the sense that
A is in a documentary that B is filming.**

A: I don't really come up here anymore.

NAME1 does – NAME2's Dad – he's up here a bit I
think.

And his brothers – they come out here and. They keep it
going but.

.

I can see the appeal – it's practical isn't it – it's.

.

there's a pragmatism I can get my head around and I
think the physical effort. Digging. Using your hands.
Something about the soil and pulling things out and
putting things out it's.

Therapeutic I.

.

I just. I don't want anything to [do with it].

.

He always wanted pets. I'm not an animal person – he
um. He'd take what he could get – kept stick insects and
caterpillars – and then when he got this place he'd keep
chickens.

Give us the eggs, you know.

.

We've not um. We've still got the um the.

Whatever it is they give you at the.

Ashes or. Bits of bone or – sometimes I think we should just throw him over here. On his fucking potato patch – I think he'd not mind you know.

Definitely – if it made something Grow I reckon he'd be dead pleased actually I.

.

His Dad – NAME1 wants to take a boat.

You know.

Sea.

Chuck them over the side. Sing a song. Drink beer. Hold hands. Shout Poems at the sky. Imagine him on the fucking waves forever I.

.

I don't think he gave a shit about the sea to be honest. NAME2.

.

Is this [right]? Is this the sort of thing you're [after]?

B: This is great, 'A'

A: .

Okay

B: Really great

A: You're just saying that

B: It's lovely to hear you talk about him

A: saying that so I'll keep talking

B: .

A: I'm not wrong

B: Of course I'd like to help you keep talking if you'd like to keep talking

A: Help me?

B: .

Does it help you to talk about your son?

A: .

[don't know].

B: In this space. This really beautiful place that he loved?

A: .

Did he love it?

You're talking about him loving it as though you knew that he loved it.

B: .

Didn't he?

A: .

No idea.

.

*She looks at the camera – if there is a camera to look at.*

I'm not sure I could have told you what he Loved, if he was a Loving sort of [person].

When something like this happens you

*Long pause.*

Inevitably.

my fault.

I was his mother.

Am his mother.

Will continue to be his mother even as he is not here but.

And not because I feel I should have Protected him when it [happened], when she [did it].

I should have protected him when he was small because that would have protected Her and then of course him and.

well all of us really.

NAME2's Dad and I were not.

We shouldn't have had kids.

You shouldn't say that 'cos it means that your kids wouldn't be here, but really, sometimes, I think it might have been for the best 'cos what a sad fucking collection of lives.

.

B: Are you angry with her?

A: With NAME3?

B: For killing him. For murdering your son.

A: .

Yes.

No.

Maybe.

I don't know.

.

Yes. Yes, I'm fucking angry. Yes, I'm

Livid.

Yes, I Hate her, I Hate her for taking him away, for removing any potential of

.

You know. But.

.

God.

.

Do I Know her?

Do I Know that woman and what she must have felt and how Scared she was and how much she must have Hated him for what he Did to her.

Yes.

.

He used to Spit on her.

He'd piss on her.

He'd hit her in the stomach so no one asked her any questions – so the bruises weren't – I mean.

.

That's someone who's given it some Real thought. That's not an accident. That's not. Losing your temper in the heat of.

.

His Dad used to spit on me.

.

So. When I heard that she hit him with a fucking hammer. And that she kept hitting him with it – long after he'd stopped breathing. I felt like I'd been in that room with her. I felt like her. Not like him.

## 72. CODES.

**This scene is for at least one adult (A). A can be talking to as many or as few people as you like. Or to no one.**

A: 16.52 a code red on G wing. Miss N cut her arm with a razor.

20.45 hours Miss K passed a blade to a member of staff.

21.17 hours, Miss F on E wing very agitated.

At 22 hundred hours there was a code blue on F wing. Miss H had tied a ligature around her neck. November 3 and November 4 and a healthcare worker were all in attendance.

22.25 hours a code blue on E wing. Miss F had tied two ligatures around her neck. Oscar 1, November 3, November 6 attended.

At 23.11 hours assistance required for Miss R. Not responding.

At 23.26 hours a code blue on E wing. Miss W had a plastic paper lodged in her throat.

23.44 hours a code blue on G wing. Miss P had a plastic bag over her head.

23.55 hours a code blue on E wing. Miss D had tied a ligature. Requested to move to a safe cell. Relocated to X102.

23.58 hours. Code red on G wing. Miss L slashed wrists with blade, not yet located. Oscar 2, November 6 and a healthcare worker in attendance.

Zero hours thirteen a code blue on G wing. Miss D had tied two ligatures. November 3, November 4 in attendance.

.

And that concludes the events of the evening.

### 73. COMFORT.

**This scene is between two adults (A and B).**

A: Fuck off.

.

B: Can I just

A: Absolutely not

B: Please, if I can

A: Fuck off

B: I just

A: Fuck off harder

B: .

I just want One Minute

A: Don't give a shit what you want

B: I get that

A: Fuck Off Then

B: Please

A: She'll not talk to you.

B: I don't blame her

A: Go Away Then

B: I want to help

A: Could have done with that Months / ago

B: / I know I / know

A: / Fuck that – Years ago

B: I Know

A: Could have done with Help – no no no, sorry, could have done with somebody – Anybody – just Wanting to help years ago

B: I know

A: Even somebody having the Thought that they wanted to
   help

B: I know

A: Even That would have been of some fucking Comfort
   Years ago

B: .

   I know.

A: She can't leave the house without someone asking her for
   a blowjob.

B: .

A: Did you know that?

B: .

   I believe it.

   And

A: Wow

B: I Believe you

A: Thank You – Thank You So Much

B: And I really would like to help

A: How?

   .

B: Excuse me?

A: How? In what way will you be helping us?

B: .

   Well

A: Will you be moving in with us and helping her sleep at night?

B: .

A: Will you stand in front of windows when bricks come in?

Will you give all your time to my other kids 'cos she requires everything I've got?

Will you be paying our bills?

Can you get her off drugs?

Can you get her to eat?

Can you stop her from vomiting?

Can you stop them from coming into my house and dragging her out by her hair?

What Actual Tangible support will you be giving us?

B: .

I want to listen.

A: Yeah, I can't do Shit with that.

.

B: I lost my job.

A: .

D'you want some sympathy

B: No.

No.

I just. I wanted you to know that I was Fighting for you, for NAME1 – I know that it must not have felt like that, but.

I think Together we could

A: Get off my fucking doorstep.

## 74. CONFERENCE.

### This scene is for two adults (A and B) or one adult (A) and one child (B).

A: Good afternoon everybody, I'm 'A' – Detective Superintendent with the major investigations teams uh here in PLACENAME. I'm Senior Investigations Officer on this case. We're here to further discuss the uh the Disappearance of NAME1 who was last seen eight days ago on DATE of DATE leaving a local shop not far from her home in the early afternoon.

Just to ah

Repeat

some of those details that we

previously covered I

NAME1 had spent the day at home. She hadn't been in school, but was thought to be wearing the uniform. Nothing suggests that anything that happened That day was particularly out of the ordinary for NAME1. She had – as has previously been mentioned – been having some personal struggles, and occasionally felt unable to attend school. NAME1's sisters had seen her at breakfast, had tried to encourage her to attend some classes, but she decided to stay at home.

At some point, NAME1 left her home. She walked to the shop, which is approximately half a mile from her home. We have no CCTV footage of this journey – this is a rural area. What we have is footage from the shop of her entering. She attempts to purchase a bottle of vodka – but was refused. The owner of the shop says NAME1 was known to her, was wearing school uniform and was visibly distressed – her attempt to purchase alcohol seemed highly concerning, to the point where the shop owner attempted to contact NAME1's family and then did report the incident to the school.

NAME1 left the shop – she stepped out of the premises as the CCTV shows, and That remains the last sighting of NAME1.

We're appealing today, to anyone who might have seen NAME1 after 2.20 when she left the newsagent. Take a look at the CCTV again, remind yourself of her face and her uniform and her bag.

Of course NAME1 was clearly very upset and going through some personal difficulties. But she has never left home before and her family just want her home again.

B: .

Um. I'm.

I'm NAME1's sister.

We're really. We're really worried about you NAME1.

We're all really missing you and we just want to say. That. I just want to say. That.

I know it can be hard at home sometimes.

I don't think I'm supposed to say that.

But. I know it can be hard. But it's so much harder not having you there.

It hurts so much more

Not having you there and.

I know you'll be Cold and.

I promise we'll all be better people if you come home because.

You make us better and.

.

NAME1 is a kind, Normal girl and. We just want her to come home.

Please.

## 75. TILL.

**This scene is for three adults (A, B and C) or two children and one adult, or two adults and one child. B is always an adult.**

*C is crying. A has a knife or some other weapon that looks as though it could do serious harm. It's probably not a gun.*

A: Don't move

B: .

A: I won't hurt you

B: .

A: I'm not

    I don't want

    to Hurt you so

B: .

A: if if Nobody moves

Then

Nobody gets hurt

Okay

B: .

A: Okay?

B: okay

A: okay

B: okay

A: You – as well – okay

C: .

A: okay

C: I

A: if you don't Move then I won't Hurt you okay

C: please

A: Where's your phone

C: I

A: Where's your Phone

C: In my. It's in my bag

A: K.

Drop it.

C: .

A: I need you to drop your bag onto the floor

C: I just

A: stop crying I need you to just

    put your bag on the floor

C: I

A: Drop your bag

C: please

A: just drop it

    .

    okay okay and now.

    Take your coat off.

C: .

A: Take your coat off – don't – just – just – off quickly and –
    there

    On the floor.

    .

    Kick it over. There. Kick your bag and your coat come
    on – kick them over.

    .

    Stop crying.

    .

    Open the till

B: .

A: Open it

B: .

   I'm

A: Just Open it

B: it's my whole

A: Don't. Don't do that. Okay. Just.

   Nothing Bad's going to happen.

   Okay?

   Nothing Awful is going to happen to any – stop crying – Nothing – I don't want to hurt anyone but I fucking Will okay I definitely Will so can you just

   Open the till and

   Just.

   Empty it just pass it over pass it over

B: Please don't do this 'A'.

A: .

   stop crying

C: i'm

B: I'm really begging you not to do this 'A' for

A: shut up

B: for your sake for your Mum's sake

A: shut up just give me the the the

B: 'A'

A: I'll hurt her

B: .

342

C: please

A: shut up shut up shut up / shut up

B: / 'A'

A: SHUTUPJUSTFUCKINGSHUTUPSTOPCRYING

.

stop fucking Crying I don't Want to hurt you but you're Making me Want to hurt you .

B: 'A'

A: I just want you to shut up

.

I just want this to stop now.

B: .

It can stop now.

A: no it can't. no it Can't.

B: It can.

It absolutely can.

you can just

Put that down.

you can just

Sit here.

get something to drink, I can get you something to drink.

d'you want a a a Ribena or a Lemonade or a

A: no

B: or a beer or something you can pick up a beer

A: no

B: and we can all just sit down – we can let her go out and me
   and you can just sit down on the floor and have a drink a

A: no

B: a what would you like what would you like to drink

A: a vodka

B: I can open a vodka we can have a vodka this one

A: .

B: here – look – here – let Her go out and

A: I can't

B: you can you definitely can

A: if she goes she'll call the / police

C: / I won't

A: don't fucking Lie

C: I won't I promise I won't I swear I won't

A: You're fucking Lying

C: I'm not

   I'm really not

   I'll just go home.

   I've got kids – please

A: I don't care

C: okay

A: Everyone's got fucking kids

B: 'A'

A: She's got kids, I've got kids – everyone's got fucking kids –
   d'you want a congratulations – d'you think that makes
   you special – everyone's got Kids doesn't take any fucking
   Skill to Have Kids

C: My kids Need me

A: And mine don't

C: I didn't say that.

   I didn't say that.

B: 'A'.

   You don't have to do this.

   It doesn't have to be this way.

A: .

   I don't have a choice.

   I don't have a choice

   Nothing is good

   Nothing is good

   Nothing

   Nothing

   Nothing is good

B: let her go

A: .

   No.

## 76. M4.

**This scene is for three adults (A, B and C).**

*Maybe there's a camera. They act like there's a camera but there doesn't actually need to be a camera.*

A: Okay good

B: Okay

A: That's gonna be good

B: Good

A: Yeah, that's really gonna work

B: Okay great

A: Yes

B: Fucking great

C: More blush

A: Less blush

C: Okay

B: Really

A: This light is nuts

B: Great

A: Less peppy more, like, Sombre okay

C: Yep

A: On the cheeks

C: Yep

B: I feel like I'm sinking

A: Yeah

B: We just, we want to keep the heels

A: For sure

B: Cos I have trainers in my

A: Heels are sadder

B: right

A: Heels are more Serious

B: is that

A: Like, trainers take the piss a bit

B: sure no right

A: Sort of can't express Grief with a trainer

B: yeah no, I get that, it's just that I feel like I'm digging up a potato patch with my heel and these cost four hundred quid and I don't know how Serious I'll look if I keep sort of sinking you know

A: Okay

C: That's not a potato patch

B: Great

C: That's like, um, barely a bit of grass

B: Fantastic

C: You're a city girl

B: what

C: No, it's just. I grew up on a farm. And that particular patch of grass could not look less like a potato plant so

B: I'm fucking starving

A: This won't take long

B: Do we have any food

A: D'you see a catering tent sweetheart

C: Did you miss breakfast

A: You should never miss breakfast

B: It's four AM

A: Absolutely

B: It's four AM, no one's had breakfast

A: I had a bacon sandwich

B: good for you

A: 'C' / had porridge, didn't you

C: / I had porridge, yeah

B: fucking excellent

A: 'C' sweetheart, could you pop up and grab something for
    'B' to eat

C: .

   We're in a field off the M4

A: Yep

C: I sort of feel like there's nowhere to pop To

A: Sure okay, then we'll just have to Hang on, 'B' love, you
    good to go?

B: Yep. Yep. Jesus, fuck I'm hungover

A: Great

B: Massive one last night

C: That's why you need food

A: Good stuff

B: Got absolutely wrecked. Such a good night. NAME1, you know NAME1 – she Would not stop trying to do the splits on the dance floor and Fuck me, it was hilarious – it was like, her legs were essentially only about This far apart, like, hip width, if that, and she kept just screaming Am I Doing It Yet, Am I Doing The Splits Yet Do I Look So Good and

A: Okay we're rolling 'B'

B: I'm standing in a field just off the M4.

You can hear traffic, even now, in the quiet of the morning.

This unremarkable patch of green, this stretch of grass, is not somewhere you would ever Choose to stop.

But it Is where NAME2 took her last breath.

And not due to some tragic motorway accident. But at the hands. Of her partner. Who having repeatedly stabbed her

placed his hands

slowly and deliberately

around her neck and

A: Okay cut, that's fantastic 'B'

B: Uh huh

A: That's really great, really um Intense and

349

B: sure

A: It just

B: Yep

A: If I could give a note

B: Yep

A: It sounds a little bit like you're talking us through a recipe

B: .

Okay

A: Like, or we're at a poetry reading or something

B: right

A: At a poetry reading in a field that you've dragged us all to

B: okay

A: I'm sort of struggling to figure out Why we're going so
fucking slow, you know

B: uh huh

A: So how about we run it again

B: okay

A: From the top

B: okay

A: and we're rolling

B: I'm standing in a field just off the M4 you can hear traffic
   even now in the quiet of the

A: Yeah so I see what you're doing there

B: right

A: going at twice the speed

B: because

A: But of course now you sound like you've ingested helium

B: okay

A: Let's try it again and let's see if you can take us on a
   Journey

B: Yep

A: Let's travel with you

B: Yep

A: Through this field, this drab little motorway, and let's be
   in the boot of that car that NAME2 was in, half alive, half
   stabbed to death and then let's be in this field with her as
   he squeezed the life out of her, okay, and then let's go and
   get you a fucking sausage sandwich, okay my love?

B: Sure

A: Great from the top then

B: Great.


## 77. 999.

**This scene is for one adult (A). A is on the phone.**

A: hi. fuck. hi. is there – hi.

   can you

fuck.

.

can you

he's in the car

I don't know what I've

I ran I had to fucking run

he's

there was blood he's

he's in the front of the car

the car

it's

he's still in the

by the

he was gonna

I had to

he was

and I'd said

but

by the canal, it's by the canal in front of the

he was bleeding

there was blood

I

i don't remember what I

there was no

I had no

he was gonna.

## 78. SOMEONE.

**This scene is for two adults (A and B).**

A: 'B' can I call someone for you

B: .

A: Anyone at all

B: .

A: Your Mum or a friend or

B: no

A: someone who can

B: thank you no

A: sit with you

B: no

A: be here now with

B: no thank you

A: us just while we

B: no

A: Talk.

B: .

    i don't want to talk.

i don't have anything to say.

.

why didn't you get here quicker.

A: .

We respond as quickly as we can. I'm sorry it wasn't any quicker.

B: why do you have the sirens

A: so that we can Be faster

B: it's 4 o'clock in the morning and this is a cul-de-sac.

who were you trying to get past

A: .

It's how things are done.

Officers are looking for him

B: no point

A: It'd be

.

Really.

.

If you could make a statement 'B'.

B: .

last time I did that he beat the shit out of me.

he stamped on my face.

.

last time you got him, you bailed him to here.

and he came straight at me.

and he stamped on my face.

.

I'm not saying anything.

A: .

It could really Help

B: Help who

A: .

He might not Get bailed

B: .

he will.

he always does.

.

i'm here aren't I?

i'm talking to you. there's no blood. no neighbours reported anything

A: You did

B: i shouldn't have.

A: .

Those marks on your neck are pretty serious. Those look pretty serious to me.

B: .

if you get him he'll get out and he'll get me. and if you don't get him, he'll get me.

and then one day he'll kill me. and then you'll lock him up. for a bit. and then that'll be the end of it. that'll be how it ends.

## 79. PEAT.

**This scene is for one adult. Maybe two.**

*A is standing.*

A: The peat will have moved.

.

It won't actually have Moved of course, but it will look as though it has.

I think about that all the time.

It's Mapped, I have it mapped.

Not actually.

Not an actual hand drawn map to hand over.

But here. And here and here and here.

.

There is a little peak over to the West that you can see when you're stood on the pike – the rock, that's what we called the rock – that's only noticeable if you really know the shape of that bit of land, but it does, it sort of rises up out of the ground – even if you Don't know the moor you will mark it as as Odd or out of place or. Strange somehow.

Except for now of course. Ice. And snow. And little waves and mirrors of frost.

But you could give it a very good go.

It's about 300 metres from the pike. West.

.

She's down there.

.

About eight feet.

.

He dug for hours. I had her on my lap for a while.

She's like a little submarine. Bobbing where she shouldn't.

Six winters old.

I untied her wrists and her ankles. Spread her arms out. She's on her back. Swimming an upside down butterfly.

.

Nearby there is bristle bent and star hedge and bell heather like sea foam and there are six little rocks to mark the spot.

.

He was so happy. Warm all over. He was happy for weeks.

And then, it fades. And he had to go bigger.

.

She would be nineteen now.

I never think about that. I think about him. And the peat.

And now I'm never going to say another word.

## 80. SNOW.

**This scene is for two adults (A and B).**

*Outside. Night. Cold.*

A: They always Say snow and everyone freaks out and then it doesn't come

B: No

A: Not properly

B: Well no

    A Not like – it doesn't Settle does it

B: Not in the city, no

A: no

B: Not so much

A: no

B: Do you want something to drink

A: yeah

B: D'you want to choose a couple

A: thanks

B: that's okay

A: Back home it will have settled

B: yeah?

A: yeah, I hadn't thought about that

B: right

A: can I take two

B: of course you can

A: thank you – hadn't thought about that till you said, no no, it doesn't settle in the city

B: right

A: cos you're right, it doesn't

B: Well, sometimes

A: But out in the fields.

    .

B: Are you with anyone?

A: .

    NAME1 and NAME2 are down there.

B: You looking out for each other.

A: .

    bit.

    NAME1's off her face. Goes nuts if anyone gets near her bit. She's alright.

B: Do you need condoms

A: No

B: Sure

A: Sure

B: Are you being safe

A: safe

B: yeah

A: Keeps everyone away

B: What does

A: The Snow – talking about the Possibility of Snow

B: Yes

A: I think it makes people more sort of homely

B: Homely

A: yeah you know, sort of.

> Cold outside. Warm inside. Family and. Heating on and. Roast dinner or a Pie or something. Glass of wine.
>
> Not.
>
> Fuck a hooker sort of weather.

B: 'A'

A: what

B: 'A'

A: what

B: Don't do that

A: Why not

B: Don't.

.

> Have the police been out?

A: Moved us around a few times

B: Okay

A: Don't want us down near those houses

B: right

A: Fair enough

B: Well

A: Kids and families about

B: Yeah but

A: Not nice for them I guess

B: That doesn't mean that

A: One bloke wanted NAME3 – cos she's pregnant

B: Ah

A: Had his kids in the back of the car while he fucked her in the bushes over there – it's alright that people don't want to Witness that

B: Important you're safe as well

A: Mmm

B: Important you Feel safe as well

A: I mean I never feel safe I don't know what Safe feels like I couldn't really describe that to you so I don't know why you keep using that word.

        .

B: Shall I come back later. See how you're doing.

A: No.

B: Why don't you head home.

A: Haven't made enough yet.

B: Okay.

A: Another tenner and I'll have enough.

B: .

Okay.

.

A: Back home, the snow will have settled. Up on the hill, by
the house and the shed. There will be ice, sitting above the
water.

The sheep will be up. On the highest hill.

And the cows nearer the house.

So you can look out the window at them.

### 81. FAS.

**This scene is between two adults (A and B).**

A: There are some difficulties.

B: Yes

A: There are going to be some real difficulties.

B: I hadn't imagined it would be easy

A: No

B: I've done this before – we've done this three times before,
it's never been Easy

A: I don't think this is like before Mrs 'B SURNAME'.

B: We've had problems – Difficulties – with all three of them

A: Of course

B: But that's not – that's just

A: Yes

B: In the Package, isn't it

A: .

B: Not Package. But.

.

A: I think this is going to be Much Much harder

B: Okay.

A: Significantly more difficult

B: Right

A: Right.

.

B: In what way exactly

A: No one would Blame you if you wanted to step back

B: Step back

A: Yes, take a step back and

   Reconsider your options

B: I don't

A: You've done a remarkable thing

B: I'm a mother

A: With those three children

B: I'm just their mother

A: It's really extraordinary

B: That I'm a mother

A: And if you decided that this just presented too many Difficulties

B: Sorry, can you stop talking in in – could you stop being quite so ah Vague – I don't.

.

I'm sorry. I just.

I don't really understand what it is that you're saying.

.

A: .

Have you heard of Foetal Alcohol Syndrome. ⁄

.

B: .

A: Is that a term you have come across

B: Of course it is

A: Okay

B: Of course I've

A: Okay

B: Sorry – are you saying

A: When a woman drinks

B: Yes

A: Throughout the pregnancy

B: Yes, I know what

A: To Excess

B: Yes I know exactly

A: So

B: Right

A: Half a bottle of vodka. Four, five cans of strong lager. Daily.

For example

B: I

A: Throughout the pregnancy

B: Sorry – Is that just an example or are you telling me that that's what The birth mother did? Specifically.

In the case of my child.

A: .

Coupled with the potential that the mother may have been a drug user

B: May have

A: Heroin and crack cocaine – yes, May have

B: You sure know how to sell a baby

A: So there may be withdrawal problems as well as the FAS

B: I

A: It's difficult to say at this stage in exactly what way she will be

B: So it's not necessarily

A: Movement and coordination problems. Something like cerebral palsy.

B: That's

A: Learning difficulties. There could well be problems with thinking, speech, social skills, memory etcetera

B: But you don't

A: Mood, attention, behavioural problems

B: Sorry, are you

A: Problems with the liver, the kidneys

B: Are you reading from a pamphlet

A: Hearing problems, vision problems, poor growth, distinctive -

B: Could you stop Listing things please, I. I get it.

A: .

B: Okay.

A: .

B: But you don't Know. Isn't that the. With this. That you don't Definitively Know.

A: It can be incredibly difficult to diagnose, certainly

B: Yes

A: And there is a wide spectrum of problems associated with alcohol consumption whilst pregnant

B: So

A: There are four key features of foetal alcohol syndrome. Finding all four is what is known as Full Blown FAS

B: You need a new name for it

A: Okay

B: If you're the one in charge of naming these kinds of
   conditions

A: We look for a weight below the 10th percentile.

B: I'm little. She can be little like me.

A: We look at facial features. The philtrum, the upper lip and
   the eye width.

B: Those are not. That is fine.

A: We look for central nervous system damage.

B: So her nerves are shot to shit. That's fine.

A: That's not what that means

B: I Know that's not what – I'm

A: Clinically significant structural neurological impairment.

B: I'm looking for a little Levity, I'm.

   .

   Struggling.

A: Which is why I'm suggesting you take your time.

B: I am Asking you

   To Look at me

   As though I have a Great Big Bump.

   A Belly.

   Full of a Baby.

   Because that is how I Feel about this child.

   .

A: Okay.

I am trying to be Clear.

.

Finally.

We look to confirm prenatal alcohol exposure.

B: .

*Shakes her head.*

A: .

B: Vodka.

Lager.

Half a bottle. Four. Five strong cans.

Four. Five.

A: The Mother is a known alcoholic

B: Every day.

A: She's been in contact with services, and drinking, since she was about 13.

She has been very upfront about how much she drank.

B: How helpful of her.

.

I'm sorry.

I don't mean that.

.

Except I do.

.

Poor Her.

Genuinely.

Poor Her.

.

A: It will never not be difficult.

.

B: That is not a reason to not love her.

The baby.

A: It will be Exhausting, depressing and painful.

B: That is true of many days for any parent

A: Realistically. This will be incredibly hard.

B: That is not a reason to send her back.

A: It will be a strain upon a family that has already had far
more strain than is fair.

.

B: What's fair for her?

A: That doesn't necessarily have to be your question

B: Where would she go

A: She might well find a placement with a family who haven't
already taken on so much

B: So much? You're calling my family So Much

A: Yep

B: And if she doesn't find a placement with a family who
desperately want her

A: Again, that doesn't necessarily have to be your job to solve

B: Are you saying I Can't do this

A: Everything would suggest the total opposite.

    I'm saying that you don't Have to.

    .

    The fact that we know, so early on is only a good thing.

B: Yes.

A: It can be incredibly stigmatising.

B: .

    Yes.

    Yes.

A: And.

    To be Frank

B: As though you haven't been frank

A: Excuse me

B: Announcing Your Frankness as though you haven't been
really fucking frank.

    My Children, my Family are a Joy to me. Not a list of
fucking Problems.

A: .

B: I'm sorry this is very

A: There is another woman Full of a Baby.

B: I.

A: You are not pregnant.

She is.

She is the one with the Bump, the Belly, the Foetus, the
Possibilities

B: I know I

A: The possibilities that she does not have access to – you
are a mother to three children and have extraordinary
privilege I am asking you to be conscious of that and
make a decision that is fair to you and your family and
this baby that is Not in your belly and to suggest that it Is
is fucking offensive to a woman who is carrying it and will
not get to raise it and despite what judgements you may
be making about how numb she might be to that pain I
can assure you she will be feeling it somewhere and it will
fucking Hurt

Somewhere.

Deeper than you can imagine it's.

.

B: It's.

.

I.

I didn't.

I.

It's.

I just want.

.

.

# 82. AUDITION.

**This scene is for three adults (A, B, C and D).**

*A camera.*

A: So what did you think?

B: .

Yeah. I. I Loved it to be honest

A: Great

B: I. Yeah. I couldn't put it down, I

A: Brilliant

B: just sort of.

It's a real Page Turner, it's really like a

A: Yeah, I think so too, that's definitely how 'C' wrote it

B: Like a proper um Thriller

A: Yes

B: Like, you um, like it's Rare to read a Script where you're like

Flicking the pages so you can just find out who the hell did it and.

Yeah.

That's really Exciting.

A: Great

B: Yeah

A: Perfect

B: Yeah. I mean. yeah.

It was a real um.

Pleasure.

.

That sounds [mad]

Given the uh the Subject but

A How do you feel about the Politics of this 'B'?

B: The

A: The fact that this is a True story

B: oh

A: That you would be playing someone Real, someone who
existed and who people have

Let's say, Strong feelings about?

B: .

Sure. I mean. I think the script 'C' – I think the text You
have written is really. Um. Respectful

C: Really

B: .

Yeah.

Absolutely. That's. For sure. I.

C: That's not always been the feedback.

B: .

Right.

A: What 'C' has done has written something genuinely
provocative. As drama Used to be, you know? In that

it Provokes us, it asks – it Demands questions of us – it Challenges

B: Definitely – yes. Definitely, I. That's absolutely what I experienced.

C: And what was your response to some of the Content

B: The content

C: Yes. Exactly. The Content.

B: .

It's Graphic. Certainly.

C: That's quite a different experience. To Read it. We're going to be Shooting it. Making it look As Real as possible. You'll be covered in blood. Your throat slashed. A pole inserted into your rectum

A: Not Actually, of course – Not Actually

C: The aim will be for it to Look as real as possible so that when the camera pans Up

And Down

Your body, we will Feel that it is real.

B: .

Yes. Sure. I understand that.

It.

I mean.

I think there's a Question. Isn't there. About.

God, we've Seen this, haven't we? We've Consumed enough of this kind of imagery to last us a lifetime. Haven't we? Aren't we a bit Tired of it, of receiving

sexualised images of murdered women, of Dead women,
whether it's in the Media or some form of entertainment –
or or documentary – I mean, we're Obsessed with
Dead Women and Sexualised Images of of of Mutilated
corpses – always Women, always dead white blonde
women – and I suppose, I think that sort of creates a kind
of um Hierarchy of victimhood – that kind of Feeds into
that and that um that makes me, well, that makes me
sort of Uncomfortable I guess, because, we shouldn't be
doing that to women – why are we Always doing that to
women, drawing these lines and divides – and well, and –
the other thing Your script, This piece of of of Drama
does is it feeds into that Femme Fatale thing as well,
you know the um the character of the uh the Girlfriend,
who Covers for him and and Lies for him – I mean, she
sort of becomes like the Main Villain, almost? – I mean,
definitely, she definitely becomes the villain of the piece,
despite the fact that he um he Murdered sort of upwards
of twenty women – and so I suppose there's all of that
going on, all of this dead dead dead women, evil evil evil
women, Madonna Whore thing – because of the prostitute
characters and the uh the fact the script makes so much of
the um the dead white blonde girl thing being – her being
a virgin – and that well, that's not that new frankly the
uh the the Constancy of it can feel like a fucking Barrage
sometimes, frankly, it can feel like just Existing as a
woman in the world is like walking fucking headfirst into a
Tsunami whilst simultaneously being expected to be super
relaxed and feminine and yourself and whatever but.

.

I think it's earned here.

I think.

Largely, it's. Those images. Feel part of the story.

C: Largely

B: Yes. Yes, largely.

Entirely.

I meant.

C: And how do you feel about Playing a dead woman.

B: .

I mean. Yes. Do you mean. Sorry, I just want to make sure – do you mean – playing her When she's dead?

C: .

No. Not Just when she's dead, I mean you'd be playing a murdered woman – a woman who in real life was brutally and savagely murdered.

B: .

Sure.

Yes.

But.

I mean.

.

She was also an Alive woman. She was also a.

Whole

Entire human being

who

.

as far as I can tell

lived a complex and

rich life

and.

.

yeah.

A: .

Well, that's great. That's really interesting.

Thanks so much for sharing your

thoughts.

Shall we read from the top?

## 83. ALIBI.

**This is scene is for four adults (A, B, C and D).**

A: This is your statement

B: Yes

A: This is the statement you provided to DS NAME on the
DATE?

B: That's correct

A: Can you just take a look at it for me

B: .

Yep.

Sure.

.

A: Do you mind if I read some of it out to you?

B: No.

Not at / all

A: / Thank you – you state that you were at home with
NAME1 from 6pm through until the following morning
when you left the house together for work.

B: That's correct.

A: And that neither of you left the house for the entirety of the
evening

B: That's right.

A: And you're sure about that

C: Can I ask if you're coming to a point Sergeant

A: Absolutely.

I'm just wanting to really clarify

C: She's been very clear throughout

A: She has been. She's been very clear and she's been very
helpful. I'm just asking her to keep that up for a bit longer.
We're talking about murdered children, I'm sure everyone
wants to be as helpful as they possibly can.

B: I came home from work at just before 6. I remember
because when I opened the front door I was surprised –
the radio was on and it was those um, the what do you call
them – the beep beep beep

C: The pips

B: Exactly, the pips and I thought – for the news, you know –
and I thought that I must've left the radio on when I left in
the morning – I was the last to leave that morning – and

then I thought, but, no, I don't listen to uh to Radio 4,
I – particularly not in the morning, I can't Stand all that
Shouting with my uh my cereal, anyway – so I'm really
sure of the time.

He called out and I was Surprised because I thought he'd
be back later, he was usually back Much later.

A: That's really helpful.

B: We cooked some food together. We watched some telly. We
went to bed.

A: And could he have left when you were in bed.

B: .

  No.

A: You're sure about that

B: We had sex.

A: All night?

B: I'm a light sleeper.

A: .

  And why Was he back so early?

B: .

  Change of shift?

  I don't know. I didn't Interrogate him about it – I was just
  pleased about it. He Often works nights, it's nice when he
  doesn't. I really love him.

A: Sure. Sure.

  .

  You've called the police on him a few times.

I mean.

I've seen him kick your head in.

C: How is that relevant

B: Are you punishing Me for that

A: Not at all. Far from it.

B: Plenty of people have problems.

I love him.

I think he's wonderful.

A: I think he's manipulative and charming and controlling.

And I think you're lying for him.

C: Do you have anything to back that up.

A: I'm just talking to 'B' right now

C: Doesn't work that way

A: I'm just asking 'B' one last time if she'd like to take this
opportunity to amend her statement.

B: .

No.

Thank you.

We were in all evening.

We ate pasta. We cooked together. We listened to the
radio. We watched telly – a series on Netflix we'd not
finished and then I had a bath and he chatted to me and
we drank wine and then we had sex – three times – and
then we went to sleep.

A: .

Okay.

.

I wonder whether you've got to that point where you're so invested in the lie that you believe it

B: I'm not lying

C: Can you wrap this up

A: Three children have been murdered.

B: .

Not by NAME1.

A: .

Your Mum came in this morning.

B: .

No she didn't.

A: .

She told us you were with her that evening. That you'd had a row with NAME1. He'd put his hands around your throat again. He'd pinned you up against a wall and he'd spat on you. You'd driven to your Mum's and you'd stayed there for the night. She was hoping – as she hoped every time you did that – that you would leave him.

You had a bath there. She made you pasta, but you couldn't eat it as your throat was so swollen. He didn't call – which she found unusual – normally, when you came to hers, he would harass and abuse her and you with phone calls and threats and texts and demands before apologising and begging and you would always return before morning.

This behaviour that deviated from the norm, unsettled your Mother but also gave her some hope.

You slept in her bed, as you always did on those visits home.

In the morning, you hadn't heard from him and were beside yourself.

She begged you not to go.

You pushed her back. Bruised her elbow. She fell and cut her head. You insisted you were returning to him.

She said you weren't to come to her again until you really were ready to leave.

.

She remembers the date very precisely because the cut on her head wouldn't stop bleeding so she went to the hospital.

.

And as soon as she heard about NAME2 and NAME3 going missing and the name of your village mentioned. She said she felt sick.

.

And then of course, three days later NAME1 turns up on her doorstep and tells her that if she tells us that you were with her, he'll kill her in her sleep, just as soon as he's killed you.

.

You must be terribly frightened.

I understand that.

A: .

B: Every single day

It gets worse.

A: Yes I've noticed.

B: Then what are you going to do about it

A: What do you Suggest I do about it

B: .

Hire more staff

A: Oh excellent, yeah, I'd not thought of that one 'B' that's really brilliant

B: It's not My Job to come up with solutions – it is literally yours. That's why you get paid about six times what I get paid

A: Way off

B: I'm Telling you that I'm not doing it.

I'm not going to do any of it.

I will not attempt and fail to make forty five meaningful observations in an hour. Not doing it.

A: So what are you proposing?

You do None of them.

B: Exactly.

A: So None of these women get help. That's your solution.

B: It's not a solution.

It's a protest.

A: I mean it's a really fucking shit idea – have you got an aspirin

B: No.

Women will Die.

I know you think I'm being.

But.

Women will die

A: I don't think you're being.

.

Of course I don't.

I Know that.

I'm on your fucking side.

I just Have nothing – I can just Do nothing.

B: I don't believe you.

A: Falsify the record.

B: .

What did you say.

A: Do as many as you can.

And then falsify the record.

B: Are you still drunk

A: Possibly – it's possible. But. That, so far has been the solution

B: So far

A: Yep, that's what people have done. That's what we've
– what I have encouraged people to do in these
circumstances, so. That's what I'm encouraging you to do.

B: .

Fucking hell.

A: .

Mmmm.

.

I'm just going to.

.

to.

take the edge off.

.

B: My objection to it was not administrative.

I'm not Raising this because it is administratively
complicated for me – because I fear the repercussions on
my record if I don't hit all my targets – my bringing this
to your attention was because I cannot stand in front of
forty five different women and get a clear picture of their
mental wellbeing and their likelihood to commit an act
of self harm – particularly given the pool of women we're
talking about have a History of self harm and suicidal
thoughts – I cannot Do that giving, what, two minutes per
woman?

A: .

Yeah, I understand that 'B'. I just need you to catch up a
bit. Get past the moral outrage stage and come join me up
here with trying to work with what we have. Within our

capabilities and with what resources we Do have – which, as you've successfully identified – are fuck all. You can do your protest and feel excellent about it, or you can come and get your hands dirty and Attempt To Do Your Job. To stand in front of them and give them Something. And Hope. And possibly make a difference. Or not. But, really, I sort of need you to get really fucking realistic really quickly because This, all of This isn't helping anyone except for possibly your own sense of self entitlement. And it's definitely making my hangover a shit ton worse.

So.

Yeah.

Crack on I reckon.

## 86. SWAB.

**This scene is for three adults (A, B and C).**

*A has double, non sterile gloves on and evidence bags. C is a police officer. C watches. Perhaps B is covered in blood.*

A: If you open wide for me, I'm just going to place a swab inside your cheek, okay?

B: .

A: That's great, nice and wide.

B: .

A: Thank you, you can close.

B: .

A: I'm just going to change gloves, if you bear with me.

B: I didn't do anything.

A: .

B: I know they're saying I did it, but I didn't – I would never – I'm not that kind of person.

A: Okay, can you hold out your hands.

B: .

A: I'm just going to take some swabs underneath your fingernails, okay?

B: .

I didn't do anything.

A: Hold still please.

B: I'm telling the truth

A: Okay

B: I wouldn't Hurt somebody like that

A: Okay

B: It's not in my Nature in my

A: Okay

B: Capacity

A And just keep that hand like that for me

B: I didn't do it

A: Hold still please

B: .

I didn't do it.

I wouldn't do it.

I've never hurt anybody. I wouldn't hurt anybody.

Particularly not.

You know?

That's.

Unthinkable.

That's.

I couldn't.

I just.

A: Okay.

All done.

B: I didn't do it.

I didn't do anything.

## 87. RESTAURANT.

**This scene is for two adults (A and B)**

A: I'm really sorry.

B: .

A: I should've called.

B: .

A: I've been stood outside for about twenty minutes.

B: .

What.

A: I didn't realise it had been that long, I just.

When I got here, I couldn't come inside and.

B: What d'you mean you couldn't come inside

A: I just.

I just Couldn't, I just Felt like I couldn't Move.

B: .

Could you sit down please.

A: .

B: You're an hour late, I feel Humiliated, could you sit down
please.

A: .

I'm really sorry.

B: .

Then I'll go

A: .

No, I'm.

.

I'm really sorry.

B: .

What happened.

A: I.

B: I'm So Angry with you.

I know something has happened, I assume something
Completely Awful has happened and That is why you
are so late and you're being so fucking Nuts, but before
you tell me and it has to be all about that, I just want to
say I am Fucking Furious with you. I feel like I can barely
Breathe I'm so angry.

A: .

    I know.

    I'm so sorry.

B: Things have been Awful.

A: I know.

B: For Such a long time

A: I know

B: And Largely that has stemmed from you being Thoughtless

A: I know

B: And Cruel

A: .

    I know

B: And Self Involved

A: I know

B: .

    But now I look like the Dick here because as ever – I am doing all the talking and you are just sitting there like you've been hit by a car.

A: I wanted to let you speak

B: Why are you Always the victim?

    Why do you Always get to be the victim?

    .

A: Someone killed themselves today.

B: .

A: An inmate.

B: .

A: I found them.

B: .

A: And it was my fuck up. Entirely mine.

B: .

    I'm sorry.

A: She's been asking for help, I know that she has been asking
for help and she's. I've been. I have been Meaning to get to
her but because she is quiet I just haven't got there yet and.


    .

She hanged herself in her cell and she was on a list

of of

meaningful observations and.


    .

No one got to her – she was in there for over an hour
before.


    .

I'm Good at my job.

I Care about those women.

I Value them and their lives and.


    .

Fuck it, I believe in Rehabilitation, I Genuinely believe in
rehabilitation but.

What are we doing?

What's the Point anymore, I.

.

I'm sorry.

I'm done, I'm. I'm here.

B: .

I'm sorry that that happened.

A: Thank you.

B: I'm sorry that she died.

A: Yes.

B: .

I ordered for you.

A: Yes.

I'm not hungry.

B: .

No.

Okay.

Fine.

*B eats. A does not.*


## 88. RESTRAIN.

**This scene is for at least five adults.
Eight would be better.**

A: Calm down

B: I Am Calm

A: You don't seem calm 'B'

B: I mean it feels a lot like you're trying to Make me not /
   calm

C: / Can you just try some deep breaths for me there please
   ·'B'

B: Fuck's sake

C: Just try and stay still okay

B: I Am Still, you're the ones fucking circling me like like
   fucking pigeons or

D: We need to get you back in your room 'B' and we can have
   a chat

B: I don't want to have a chat

D: Okay, that's fine

B: Can you just fucking step Back a bit I feel like I can't /
   Breathe

A: / We're standing at an Appropriate distance 'B'

C: We're here for your safety

B: Yeah it doesn't Feel like that

D: You need to stop raising your voice

B: I'm fucking not raising my voice

C: It feels like you're being quite aggressive 'B'

B: I'm Pissed Off you've wrecked my fucking room

D: That's not what's happened 'B'

B: Yeah it is – Look at it

A: You know why we had to do that

B: Fuck off you didn't have to

A: You Know we had to 'B' – we have to remove things if you're going to harm yourself

B: Why doesn't anyone just come and have a Conversation with us / why do you have to Wreck my room

C: / That's what we're doing – we're trying to have a / conversation with you

B: / Before you fuck up my room – how about we have the chat Before you fuck / up my room

D: / We're just trying to keep you Safe 'B'

B: Stop fucking saying that

C: Since NAME1 left

B: Oh fuck off

C: We know it's been difficult for you

B: Shut up

A: Can you just Try and take a deep breath

B: D'you know what if you fucking Backed Off a bit maybe I Could / Take A Deep Breath

A: / 'B'

C: / Come on / now

B: No you're Winding me up you're fucking / Doing it on purpose

D: / 'B' come on

B: Just Step Back a bit and give me a bit of / breathing space

C: / We're a really appropriate distance okay 'B'

B: Just Fuck Off

C: Okay

B: Fuck The Fuck Off

D: Alright now

B: GetTheFuckAWAYfromme

> *B makes a move – a small move, but a gesture she hasn't yet made and suddenly the others are on her. They restrain her effectively and quickly as she struggles against it – but it looks painful and it sounds painful – she cries out. They hold her still and press down. She begins to cry.*

B: NO

A: Alright alright alright

C: It's okay

D: Breathe

B: getoffme

C: It's okay

B: no

D: It's okay

B: stop it I can't breathe

A: It's alright

B: please

A: It's alright

B: I want my Mum

C: I know

A: It's okay

B: it hurts

A: It's okay

B: it hurts

A: It's okay

B: it hurts

A: It's okay.


## 89. LOCK.

**This scene is for two adults, or one adult (B)
and one child (A).**

A: I'm sorry.

B: You don't have to say sorry to me sweetheart.

A: .

> Don't say I only have to say sorry to myself. That's so
> much worse.

B: No.

> I don't mean that.
>
> I imagine that's already happening on some level.
>
> I mean. You can say sorry to those poor people til the end
> of your days I think

A: I have

B: I know you have

A: I feel awful

B: I know you do

A: I didn't want to upset anyone

B: I know

A: I didn't want to hurt anyone

B: I know

A: I should have picked somewhere further away

B: 'A'

A: I should have. I hate the idea of Mrs NAME1 being scared.

B: She's very kind. She asks after you whenever I go into the shop.

A: Does she

B: It's not okay to scare Anyone 'A'. It's not okay to put Anyone through what you put those poor women through

A: I know

B: She can't sleep. That poor woman. She can't sleep at night because of what You did

A: I know

B: I go in that shop every day.

I spend an obscene amount of money in that shop every day trying to make it up to her I think.

Got packets and packets of biscuits and mountains of tinned food that nobody will eat just piling up at home.

I had to Reclaim it I think.

A: .

That sounds like a good thing to have done.

.

I don't regret it though.

B: .

A: I don't. I know you want me to say I do, but I just don't.

I needed to come back.

I needed to get clean.

They know me here. They're nice to me.

I needed to do something bad enough to come back. For long enough that I could stay. Get clean again. Sort myself out.

B: This is not the only way to do that.

A: I know you say that but it Is.

B: I could have helped you.

You could have let me help you.

A: It never worked.

The closest you ever got was locking me in.

Turns out they do that here. And it's easier. Cos no one loves me here. I'm not hurting anyone here when it's hard.

B: You don't know that

A: You couldn't do it.

And that's okay.

'Cos you're not supposed to be able to do that – that bit isn't in the normal parenting bit. Is it.

B: There are other ways 'A'.

You have hurt people.

You have damaged people's lives.

A: I know.

But I was going to die.

I was going to end up dead.

And this way, I get to live.

And you get to keep me.

## 90. DOG.

**This scene is for two adults (A and B).**

A: Excuse me

B: Yep

A: Can you

B: Yep

A: Just hang on a second I'm

B: yeah, no I'm just

A: it's really hard to Talk to you when you're walking away

B: Yeah I'm just in a rush so

A: Sure it's

B: So I

A: won't take long and my leg is knackered so can you

B: Your leg is knackered

A: I had an accident last week

B: I'm sorry to hear that

A: could you

B: should you be working if you had an accident last week

A: It was minor, it wasn't a big

B: Okay well if it was minor I'm just gonna keep

A: could you not

B: cos I've got shit to do

A: I'm sure

B: and you Following me is

A: sure

B: Pissing me off a bit now

A: right

B: is this something you do to Everyone who comes in your
    shop or

A: no I

B: am I particularly lucky to have been selected for some kind
    of escort you round the fucking supermarket – your leg is
    bleeding

A: I mean I said

B: yeah but it's really bleeding

A: I had an accident

B: you said minor

A: it Was minor

B: doesn't look fucking minor you're pissing blood all over the

A: in the grand scheme of things, it Was minor

B: grand scheme of

A: like in comparison to what it Could have been, what kind of accident it Could have been

B: right

A: like a – like I didn't get hit by a car or

B: that's

A: have it Crushed by a tractor or

B: insane, that's an insane thing to say

A: Comparatively, the accident could have been Much worse

B: I mean, that doesn't make any sense – that's a ridiculous way to go through life

A: I find it quite helpful – would you mind emptying your bag please.

B: .

what did happen. To your leg.

A: .

Dog.

B: Dog.

A: Dog bit it.

B: Ouch.

A: Really. Clamped down its jaws and fucking shook it.

B: Fucking ow.

A: .

B: You should take some time off. For that.

A: .

   I can't afford to.

B: .

   Right.

   .

A: Could you.

   Would you mind just opening your bag.

B: .

A: Or.

   Could you just.

   Maybe return to Aisle Seven. And.

   Put that stuff back.

B: What stuff.

A: The stuff in your bag.

B: .

A: And I'll leave you to it.

B: .

A: And then you can get going.

B: .

A: And that'll be it.

B: .

    i can't afford to.

A: .

    right.

    right.

    no.

    i mean.

    no.

## 91. GOODBYE.

**This scene is for three adults. (A, B and C).**

*A camera – as though a documentary is being filmed. Maybe C is not onstage, maybe they are and they are holding the camera.*

*B is packing. A sometimes helps, but is mostly talking to the camera. B smiles a lot.*

A: She's going to be great

B: .

A: I'm so proud of her, I can't tell you

B: stop it

A: No, no way.

    She's done Amazingly here – like. Complete life turnaround, you know

B: So've you

A: Not the same. No way.

I've got all this Support on the outside, you know. I've got people who come and visit me Every week – family and mates who fight over who gets to come and see me – like, I'm not joking

B: She's not

A: I've got So many people rooting for me, you know

B: It's really nice – they Love her so much

A: She's met them all

B: .

A: They love her too

B: .

A: My Mum's like – Best thing that ever happened to you, that girl.

B: She's a really nice Mum.

A: 'Cos, actually, No one from my family has been inside before

B: .

A: And that's pretty unusual actually

B: yep

A: So, 'B' – right, 'B' was born here

C: .

    As in TOWNNAME?

B: Nope

A: No – she was born In here, Inside This prison. Like, right here.

I mean, not Literally here, but on the on the mother and baby wing

Isn't that

Nuts?

B: My Mum was a drug addict and a repeat offender – she had me on her third time inside

A: Isn't that Mad

C: Wow

B: So

A: So this is like, this is actually her Home

B: I mean

A: No place like home

B: ha

C: So

Do you have memories of it 'B'?

B: You mean from when I was a baby?

C: Yeah.

B: .

No. We left – me and Mum together – when I was about 1.

There are photos though.

.

And then this has been my fourth time here since then.

A: no place like home

B: But my Mum hasn't been back

A: yeah

B: So that's good

A: yeah

B: And we don't. She doesn't talk to me. My Mum. Which is
sort of [hard].

But also.

Fair enough

A: No

B: Yeah I mean. They tell you all the time, like. Company you
keep isn't it. Like, don't hang around with people who are
just in and out if you want to stay clean and she wants to
stay Clean and / I respect that

A: / Hang around with though – she's your Mum

B: Yeah but.

Hard for her.

I get it.

A: I think she's a dick.

B: And.

Well.

Fuck it, I hope this is my last time

A: It is

B: But, it's hard cos. There's a bit of me just going, you'll be
back. You know?

A: Don't though

B: I mean, you try not to but

A: Course

B: It's like. A revolving door I guess. It feels really hard to get away from all the things that mean you just come back here

A: You've got to think positive

B: I know

A: You've got to have hope

B: Yeah

A: We've got a plan

B: Yeah

C: What's the plan

A: She's gonna get a flat

C: Right

A: And a job

B: .

A: And a dog

B: I'm not getting a dog

A: She is she's going to get one of those Massive ones – what're they called

B: She means a Great Dane and I'm not getting one

A: She is and she's going to call it NAME1 and it's going to be big enough to give me pony rides

B: .

   they don't do / that

A: / Then I'm gonna get out and I'll come to the flat and I'll get a job and I'll look after NAME1 and we'll live happily ever after.

B: .

Quite hard to get a job.

These days. Isn't it.

A: There are always jobs.

C: What did you do before 'B'?

B: .

I mean I sold crack. And I worked on the street.

C: You mean prostitution

B: .

Yeah. I mean prostitution.

A: She's not going back into that

B: .

The thing that's difficult is like. I come from a small place. Everyone knows me. Everyone expects me to fuck up. My Mum won't be waiting for me out there. Last three times, the first person who's come to pick me up or welcome me home is my dealer.

So.

That's just hard.

A: Yeah but. You don't give them the Satisfaction.

You do better than they Expect you to do and you get happy that way.

B: .

A: .

B: Yeah.

Yeah, it's just.

That Sounds good doesn't it.

.

I'm just.

I think.

.

The closer you get to it, the more.

Like.

Impossible.

It all feels.

Like.

You just Know.

You're going to Try your hardest.

You're going to push up against it all

As Hard as you possibly can.

But it's.

Sort of Immovable.

.

There's something.

About the

Inevitability of

it of.

Failing.

That sort of feels

Like it perfectly sums up Who I Am.

And I think I sort of don't know what to do about that.

## 92. GRANDKIDS.

**This scene is for two Adults (A and B).**

A: Hi

B: Hi.

   .

A: I was wondering if you could help me.

B: .

A: I know it's been.

   And I haven't.

   But.

   .

   I think I really need some help.

   .

   With the kids.

   With the.

   .

   Just.

   Maybe for a bit. Maybe you could have them for.

An hour or two.

Just so I could sleep?

.

I know I've.

.

I know You said.

.

But

.

They're your grandkids and
I think they'd love to see you and

.

I'm a bit on my knees here I'm a bit on my last.

.

Someone called the.

.

Social.

.

They came and.

.

I'm just a bit on my last.
I.

I know you really hate me I know I'm the last [person] you want to – and I know I fucked up I just.

.

I'd really appreciate it I'm.

.

I'm just really tired.

## 93. REFUGE.

**This scene is for two adults (A and B).**

A: Sweetheart you can't come in

B: .

A: I'm really sorry.

B: .

A: I'm really sorry – I said – on the phone

B: My kids are in the car

A: .

'B'

We can't – we haven't got the room

B: .

He's going to get us you know that if you send us away, he's going to kill us.

A: .

B: My kids

A: I'm sorry.

I'm really sorry

B: Please

A: There is nothing I can do – we haven't got the / beds

B: / I just drove for four hours to get here

A: I'm really sorry.

I told you on the phone – we don't have the space

B: We don't need much

A: We don't have it

B: Just Walls – that's it – just some Walls and a roof and
somewhere he can't get to us

A: I'm really sorry

B: I need help

A: I know

B: They need help

A: I know

B: Please

A: There's nothing to.

There's Nothing I can do

It's not. This is Not

something we can Negotiate

.

I'd have to Remove a family in order to accommodate
yours

B: Then do that.

Then do that.

Yep

Remove a

.

He's going to kill us.

.

We haven't got anywhere else to go.

.

Someone in there, someone in there – Everyone in there –
must have it better than we do and can Swap because
Nothing is worse than what we've got, Nothing is worse
than him

A: That's not

B: I know.

.

Can we just come in.

For just a.

Just so they can.

Have a drink of.

.

A: I can't do that.

.

I can't let you in and then make you all leave again. I
can't.

It's not fair on you or your kids or the residents.

I'm really sorry.

I'm really really sorry.

B: .

I don't know what I'm going to do.

.

My kids.

.

Um.

.

Okay.

.

Thank you.

Thank you anyway for your.

.

## 94. PSYCHIC.

**This scene is for at least four adults (A, B, C and D), but more would be fine.**

*Maybe we are outside. And maybe A has no shoes on.*

A: She's close.

.

She's really close. I can feel her. She's quite far below us. But she's at peace – she is at peace – she wants you to know that. She says she's tired, the pain – the Trauma of what happened – that has left her feeling an exhaustion, but she also says she feels a lightness. She's okay. She knows it's over. She knows that she will never know pain again. She wishes your pain would go though – she desperately wishes your pain would go, okay, that's really important – she's – gosh, she's almost Shouting that at me! – that's how important it is that you really Hear that okay – that's really – that's the Most important thing.

B: Did it hurt?

A: .

Yes. Yes, I'm afraid it did, I'm sorry. Yes, I'm afraid it hurt a great deal. But – it's not hurting anymore – she's not in any more pain – and she knew that you loved her.

Right at the end, she Knew how much you loved her and she thought about that – that was what she kept focused on when it got to the end okay – she thought of you and how much you loved her, it's very important you know that.

B: She wasn't angry

A: No

B: She didn't

She didn't feel like I'd

Abandoned her or

A: No

No.

She knew that.

She knew that the People doing this to her

C: People

A: Yes. People. She Knew that they were Awful people. She knew that it was Them. That they had taken her from you and that you loved her – she understood that.

C: .

Is she saying anything else About the people.

A: .

yes. yes. it's coming.

C: Or about Where exactly she is

A: she says we're so close

C: .

Rough ballpark

D: 'C'

A: .

It's very dark where she is. That's what she says. We have to go in a little more.

And then down. That's what she's saying.

.

C: Is she talking in metres or

A: She says the woman had Kind eyes.

.

She said that Man didn't. She said the Man had cold eyes.

And that his fingers were long.

And that he pulled her hair.

B: oh God i can't

A: She says she loves you. She says she loves you so much.
She says she knows she'll see you again.

And that she loves you.

## 95. BLOSSOM.

**This scene is for two adults (A and B).**

A: Hello 'B'.

B: .

Hi.

A: How are you feeling today?

B: .

It's sunny.

A: Yes.

It is, you're right.

.

B: It hasn't been.

It's been very dark.

A: Yes. It has.

B: There will be blossom on the trees

A: Which trees 'B'

B: .

Just. Trees.

I think I was thinking of the ones on our road. There are
three cherry trees in a row.

They're very pretty.

A: .

Your face is bruised.

B: Yes.

A: Did you want to talk about that.

B: No.

A: .

What did you want to talk about today.

B: .

After.

After the

.

Soon, I won't see you again. Will I?

A: What do you mean.

B: You're here to

Write a report.

Make an assessment.

A: That's right.

B: On my mental health.

A: Sort of.

B: You'll tell the court

You'll write something and then you'll tell people what I'm like.

A: .

  In some ways, yes.

B: And you'll make an Assessment on

  My state of mind

  .

  At the time of the.

  .

A: Yes. Yes, that's right.

B: I'm.

  .

  I'd like to be helpful.

A: Okay.

B: I'd like to help you do that.

A: Okay.

B: You must feel an enormous.

  Pressure.

A: .

B: I don't mean that in a.

  I've just been thinking about it because.

  You have to Make clear something that is impossible to
  clarify.

  You have to

  Summarise a human being or

A Moment in time that

Cannot really be summarised and

Not just for

You're not just doing that for

For

.

But so that people can Assess? Or judge or.

.

You have to reduce something that cannot be reduced.

A: .

B: I still don't remember anything.

A: .

B: There were voices. Whispers.

There had been for weeks.

.

I don't.

But.

I don't remember Words or.

Instructions.

Just.

Sounded a bit like paper. rustling. and.

I was tired.

I was really tired I don't.

And.

I was depressed and.

.

I don't want to.

I'm not trying to pretend that I was Mad or

.

that it wasn't in my control I

.

It's my fault that they're dead.

.

I just remember.

The blood.

And that NAME1 was in the bath. Face down. And I remember thinking, well, gosh, that's strange because NAME1 doesn't like baths, NAME1 never wants to do bathtime, it's always a struggle so why has he gotten into the bath on his own and laid down.

.

But I was soaking, I was wet as though I'd. Swam in my clothes and.

.

There was blood everywhere.

.

I remember standing in their bedroom and there was blood

All over the walls

And the floor

And the two of them

Lying in the middle of the room

Wrapped around one another like

I couldn't tell which leg belonged to which of them and

little round cheeks squashed up against each other and

I remember thinking.

Gosh.

NAME2 must have cut herself. And NAME3 wanted to kiss it better.

.

I can't remember picking up the knife.

I can't remember if they screamed.

I can't remember pushing NAME1 under the water and holding him there.

I can't remember the last time they said Mummy.

I can't remember whether NAME1 saw me stab the girls.

I can't really remember what they looked like Before.

When I remember them they are upside down in the bath blue and tulip red on the floorboards pressed together like flowers and

That's Hard because they don't look right, that's not how they are supposed to look.

.

And I don't have any photos because it's too painful.

.

They said they screamed.

Not the children.

People. Afterwards. Reported screams. And shouts of Mummy.

So they must have.

So it must have been me.

.

And whilst. I don't Know why.

.

I also Do know. It is Unfathomable. Unimaginable. Too bright to look at but also.

Logical.

.

Because I was exhausted.

And I couldn't cope.

And I was sad.

And they were loud.

And I couldn't figure out how to care for them.

I couldn't get it right, it was like putting the wrong clothes on or getting lost Constantly somewhere you ought to Know in your bones and

I Knew what was coming for them

I Knew life wouldn't be kind to them

How could it be

It had all been awful, nothing had been good.

.

It's so cruel. It's so awful.

.

Of course I killed them.

Of course I did.

It was the only thing To do.

Wasn't it?

It was the right thing.

Wasn't it?

It was the best thing for them really.

Wasn't it?

Ending the suffering.

Stopping the potential of any more pain.

Wasn't that the right thing to do in the end?

## 96. ALCOHOL.

**This scene is for four adults (A, B, C and D).**

A: Okay, are we ready to continue.

B: Can I have some water please.

C: There's some to your left.

B: .

Thank you.

.

A: So on the morning of the DATE of DATE, you visited NAME1's property.

B: That's correct.

A: And you made that visit on your own.

B: Yes, that's right.

C: You were late, is that

B: Yes. Yes, I was.

C: And why was that?

B: Um. I was. I was Often late. I had a huge amount of casework and I wasn't keeping on top of it. The Specifics that day, I don't. Recall.

A: Had you visited NAME1 before?

B: Yes. Once.

This was a follow up.

D: And you'd been alerted to her case by her / mother

B: / Her mother, yes that's right.

Her mother had contacted us several times, feeling particularly anxious for the welfare of the three children.

D: And why was that

B: She had a history of drug abuse. Self harm and depressive episodes. She tended to Engage with services and then fall away in patterns. See a doctor, seek help, take medication. And then refuse to keep in contact.

They moved a great deal as a family. She'd been in
PLACENAME for

six months.

C: And how did you find things on this particular visit.

B: .

She was anxious. Tired. She didn't have much support –
the relationship with her mother was not entirely
positive – the mother had terrible anxiety.

The house was a little.

Not messy. There wasn't enough In it to call it messy.

The children seemed pale. Tired. A little undernourished
perhaps.

It didn't feel

Urgent.

Alarming.

D: It didn't feel alarming that the children seemed
undernourished

B: Most of the children I encounter are undernourished in
some form.

A: .

Less than two hours after you left, those children were
dead.

B: .

I believe that's correct, yes.

A: .

When the police first visited the scene, they reported a higher level of neglect than you're suggesting.

B: .

A: Evidence that the children weren't washed properly. Nappies unchanged.

No bedding.

Not Enough beds, in fact – it seemed that the three children slept in one cot – did you visit the bedrooms.

B: I.

I can't recall.

C: Why is it that you can't recall

B: As I say, I visit many properties and

C: One would assume that this one might Stand out in your memory. Given what followed.

B: .

I didn't look at the bedroom, no.

D: And why was that.

B: I was in a rush.

D: Because you were late

B: Yes.

And because of the workload.

.

C: Do you drink alcohol, 'B'.

B: .

Yes.

C: To excess?

B: .

On occasion.

C: Do you drink in the daytime.

B: .

Sometimes.

C: Or the morning.

B: .

.

.

I have done.

C: Had you had a drink that morning.

B: .

.

It's possible.

C: Possible ·

B: Probable.

C: .

Your colleagues describe you as often smelling of alcohol.

B: .

Okay.

C: Do you think it's possible that NAME1 would have noticed
that.

B: I.

I can't say.

Perhaps.

I'd have thought it was unlikely.

She seemed a little

Out of it.

Catatonic

A: Catatonic

B: That's not the word I

That's too Severe I just.

I think she was a little consumed with her own problems
to observe mine.

A: So it was a problem

B: That I was drunk at work in the morning? Yes, I'm
conscious that that was a problem.

.

I don't believe it caused the death of those three children,
however.

A: No.

Nobody has implied that it did.

B: She was clearly going to do that anyway.

A: That's impossible for us to say.

Though I daresay that will occupy you.

.

C: Do you remember anything that she said to you. Whilst you were there.

B: .

Not really. Not any specifics.

She said she was tired.

` .

C: She has talked about you a great deal.

B: .

C: She has said she begged for help.

B: .

I don't recall.

C: She says that 'A Woman arrived. A woman I can't remember if I dreamt or not. A woman in a shirt and a red red mouth. A woman who looked at the children and smiled, and looked out of the window and said 'what a lovely view' and I thought at that point that I must be imagining her because the window overlooked a brick wall.'

B: Right

C: Which it does. NAME1's front room faces a brick wall.

B: Right

C: She says that she begged you to take the children away from her right then.

That it was an emergency.

That something awful was going to happen.

That she was out of control, that she was on the brink of losing control.

B: .

C: She said you squeezed her cheek.

And that you left, leaving the door open.

B: .

And that's.

You're.

You've

Decided that that is fact have you.

C: She's been awfully forthcoming.

She's distressed.

She knows what she has done.

She has no reason to lie.

B: .

I don't remember the visit happening in that way.

.

D: Would you say that things felt similar on your previous visit to NAME1? Your initial visit?

B: .

Yes.

Yes, I'd say so.

C: .

Your notes from that visit appear rather brief.

B: .

Yes.

I'm not as efficient with my notes as I ought to be,
certainly.

C: It doesn't read as though you fully inspected the property
on that occasion either.

B: .

No. I don't think I did.

D: Is it likely that you were drinking on That occasion also.

B: .

I don't know.

D: You crashed your car that afternoon.

B: .

I did.

D: Into a tree.

B: That's correct.

D: Wasn't reported until that evening.

B: That's right.

D: That's a little odd.

B: I was busy.

D: Too busy to report you'd crashed your car.

B: Yes.

D: And too late for a breathalyser.

B: .

  I suppose so.

D: You abandoned the car.

B: I did.

  That was foolish.

D: So it's possible you had been drinking.

B: .

  Yes. It's possible.

A: How do you feel when you think about this case. About
   your work on this case.

B: .

  i'm sorry i can't.

  .

  if you give me a

  .

  .

  Awful.

  Obviously.

  .

  Deeply ashamed.

  .

  It's unbearable.

  .

I can't say anything to that that will come close to.

.

But I didn't Cause this to happen.

My negligence didn't Cause this to happen.

We are understaffed and under-resourced and under-supported. No. Unsupported, unresourced, Unstaffed.

We see the worst of people. We see people Desperate and Trying and we have to make the Worst decisions. We have to encounter people at their Worst.

And that. As a job. Is unsustainable.

I am not responsible for this. I did not make this happen.

A: .

You did not stop it from happening either.

B: .

*nods.*

## 97. GROW.

**This scene is for as many people in your company as possible.**

*Outside. Bright. Everyone is planting flowers in a beautiful garden. A Child or an Adult waters them.*

# 98. SPATTER.

## **This scene is for one adult (A).**

A: We can classify bloodstain patterns into three basic types.

Passive stains, Transfer stains and Impact stains.

Passive stains include drops, flows and pools. These typically result from gravity acting on an injured body.

Transfer stains result from objects coming into contact with already existing bloodstains and leaving wipes, swipes or a pattern transfer behind. For example – a bloody shoe print or a smear from a body being dragged.

Impact stains result from blood being projected through the air and are usually seen as spatter. But may also include gushes, splashes and arterial spurts.

The characteristics of blood spatter depend on the Speed at which the blood leaves the body and the level of force applied to the blood source.

When we talk about Cast offs we're looking at the results of when an object swung in an arc flings blood onto the nearby surfaces. This occurs when an assailant swings an object back before inflicting another blow. Analysts can tell the direction of the impacting object by the shape of the spatter – tails will point in the direction of motion. Counting the arcs can reveal the minimum number of blows delivered.

Sharp force injuries, from a stabbing for example, are caused by an object with a relatively small surface area – whether with a knife or an ice pick perhaps. Less blood will be deposited on the instrument, resulting in a smaller, more linear pattern of stains.

## 99. A GRAVE.

**This scene is for two adults (A and B).**

A: .

B: .

A: You don't look the same.

B: No

A: No.

    As you did in

    there in the

    Courtroom.

B: No

A: You're taller

B: .

A: You were always hunched over maybe that's it I

B: right.

A: .

    Thank you for meeting me.

B: That's okay.

A: I don't know why I'm here.

B: That's okay.

A: .

    What do you mean.

B: .

I just think it's okay that you don't know why you're here.

A: .

You're thinner.

.

B: I'm not very well.

A: They said.

.

Maybe that's why I'm here.

B: Perhaps.

A: Your hair looks grey.

B: Yes.

A: Your face is lined.

B: Yes.

A: You're breath is thin.

B: Yes.

A: I didn't think you'd Age like normal people. Like a human being.

I assumed you were made from some other

substance

some other

.

I thought you would live forever.

.

But you just look very old.

B: .

A: Do you think about me.

B: .

No.

I don't.

A: Do you think about my daughter.

B: .

No.

Never.

A: .

She might have had children.

B: Yes.

Women do that sometimes.

A: You didn't have any.

B: No.

A: Good.

B: Yes. Probably.

A: .

I didn't have any others.

B: .

A: I couldn't.

We tried and tried for such a long time but NAME1 was all we had, but it didn't feel like that when we had her – it felt like we had it All.

B: That's nice.

A: I'm glad we didn't have others.

B: Oh.

A: They wouldn't have been able to Live after what you did. I wouldn't have let them out of my sight. They'd not know what daylight felt like on their skin.

I suppose that's what it's like for you.

B: We go outside sometimes.

There are chickens here.

And a garden.

A: I don't want to hear about that.

B: okay.

A: You stole so much.

B: Yes.

A: Did it feel wonderful.

B: .

A: I thought about snatching a child. Grabbing one whilst it played and hauling it into the car just like you did. Just to feel what you did. Just to find a little symmetry.

.

That was your bit, was it.

your main job.

You grab them.

Less conspicuous because you're a woman.

.

I wonder if anyone saw you with NAME1 and thought you were her mother.

B: .

Probably not.

I never looked very maternal.

A: .

I'm trying to look at your eyes.

I'm trying to see if they look kind.

B: .

A: Do you remember her.

NAME1.

B: .

Yes.

A: .

Do you remember her at the end.

B: .

Yes.

A: .

Was she in pain.

B: .

Yes.

A: .

Did you help.

B: .

Yes. A little. If he wanted me to.

A: .

Did she cry.

B: .

Yes.

A: .

Did you hold her.

B: .

Yes.

A: .

Were you kind to her.

B: .

I did try to be.

Afterwards.

Once she'd died.

I did feel very sorry for her in those moments.

She was very small.

A: .

Where is she.

B: .

    He knows.

A: But you were there too.

B: Yes.

A: I want to bury her.

B: We already did that.

A: .

    I want to bury her in a graveyard that I can visit so I can lay flowers. I want her to have a headstone so that everyone can see her name.

    I feel like you've still got her.

    And I feel like she doesn't exist.

    Like I dreamt her up.

    Her Dad died.

    My Mum died.

    My sister's dead.

    Maybe she was never here in the first place.

    I just want to put foxgloves on her grave.

    .

B: He knows where she is.

    .

A: Did you love him.

B: Very much.

A: Do you still love him.

B: Very much.

A: Do you write to him.

B: Every day.

A: Does he write to you.

B: No.

    Never.

    Not once.

A: .

B: It's exquisite.

    The longing.

    It's sharp.

    Breathless.

    Like freezing cold water all over your body.

# 100. DINNER PARTY.

*A big beautiful table in the middle of a kitchen. Bunches of flowers, plates of food. Mismatched plates and glasses. Water jugs. Candles in jars. Big*

*glass doors lead onto a garden. A sliding door leads to a huge kitchen. D, E, F and G are sitting at the table, drinking, eating, talking.*

*C and D live in this house, E does too sometimes. Maybe a dog wanders in and out of the space.*

*People certainly do - to refill a glass, to have a cigarette, to make a call.*

*A and B have just walked in, C right behind them having let them in. A and B still have coats on.*

*Everyone wanders in and out of the room. Everyone eats and drinks and moves around.*

*This is quick.*

*The smallest pause.*

A      This Smells Incred / ible - Hiiiiii / Everybody

D      / 'AAAAA'

E      / You're / Heeeeere

A      / I Am here I Am

D      I Told you she was coming

F      took fucking long enough / come here

A      / I know I know we're so / late

E      I knew she was coming you twats

G / I'm not standing up come and / kiss me on my cheeks

D You Did not you you kept banging / on about how she wouldn't come

C / 'B', let me take your / coat

E / shut uuuuuuup that was You

A / You all look So / beautiful and it all smells So delicious

B / thank you - that's - I can / hang it up

F / Don't cry

C Not at all, pass it here

A (shrugging her coat off and letting it just drop on the floor) I know right - that would be Peak Me - to Burst in and Sob all over you - where're

'H' and / 'I'

F / Having a fag

G 'H' is not smoking 'H' is on the loo

E Don't say On the loo

A these crisps are delicious

G why / not

C They're homemade

E it's Disgusting, say In the loo - we don't know what / she's doing

G / she's been in there for twenty minutes I think we Do know what she's been / doing

A / Oh so we're not even the last ones Here / Ideal

G / Uhhhh

F fuck off nice try

E having a fag in the garden is not the same as being an Hour / late

A     / not an Hour - we're not an Hour late - I'm sorry

C     / 'B' We've got Dogs, do you mind

B     do I mind?

C     yes are you Okay with / dogs

D     What would you say if she Wasn't okay with dogs

B     it's fine

D     take them out back and shoot / them

B     / that's / not necessary

C     / We can keep them in the kitchen

D     It's So good to / see you

A     / Isn't it though it's been forever I'm fucking Gasping for a drink - but but everyone - Everyone - This is 'B'

B     Hi

E     It's so nice to meet / you

G     / We've been Dying to meet / you

B     / Oh

A     where are the dogs

F     'I' is probably Riding them outside

B     I'm fine with dogs. Really.

A    Don't say that you'll / freak her out

C    / She produced a List of things we're not allowed to ask you about

G    She's not joking

A    You're such a bunch of cunts

H    (*entering*) That is extraordinarily rude

A    They just told her about the email / I Love You

B    / Email - what email

H    And I love and cherish You

A    You look beautiful

H    I'm wearing No make up, not a Scrap, hi, you must be 'B'

B    Hi

H    I'm 'H', nice to meet you - have you met / everyone yet

B    / Um / No

E    / She sent us all an Email last night / Titled

G    / Titled: Do Not Fuck Up The Best Thing / That Has EVER HAPPENED TO ME

F    / you're such a dweeb

G It was literally in capitals / though                    B    wow

D / And with, like, bullet points

F Like, this, Instruction Manual

H It was a really beautiful and profound / thing actually

G / We've all known her for Years and she thinks she can just sweep in and Tell us how to talk to her new / girlfriend    D    beautiful?

F / What an asshole

H Seeing someone just sort of Bear themselves like that - she likes you So Much

C 'B' let me get you a drink         B    I

B I'm. Thanks. That's

C We've got literally everything

A She's not exaggerating, this place / is fucking heaven - and I love you for changing the subject

C / There's um, beer, wine, all the spirits. All the juice. All the mixers. Ice, no ice / it's really whatever you    D    We'll be returning to it

B / I mean - I'm happy with whatever    G    Tout suite.

C Please don't be polite                    is that.

D Being polite is literally the worst thing you can do in our home    anything - did I

F We're having These

A    Fuck yes

H    They're very good

G    They're like the drink equivalent of crack

B    right

A    You like crack do you

G    I fucking love crack

I    (*entering, still smoking*) Did you actually Bring crack

A    'I'

I    Cos that'd be fucking great

A    You are Not smoking in here come here - are you actually letting her smoke in your kitchen

D    We love her, we want her to feel at home - 'B' help yourself

C    it's just a kind of cocktail thing

A    shut up please.

G    Can you Drink crack

A    Oh God they're so good

C    we make them all the time

E    Did you just ask if you can Drink / crack

D    the mint is from the garden

I    / Can you just answer the question, I feel all like, Itchy did you / bring crack

A    / No I didn't bring crack

G    I mean you Could?

I    Fuck my life. You look good

E    no. absolutely not.

A    Are you single again

E    you have fundamentally misunderstood what / crack is

I    / I'm always single, even when I was married I was fucking single, this must be your new girlfriend, hi 'B' we're all obsessed with you

A    don't say obsessed you'll freak her out I'm trying not to freak this one out

C    They've got, like berries in, from the garden 'B' - and this vodka made in um this local distillery - we're friends with the guy who / Anyway

F    / They're fucking delicious

       D    He's Swedish - the distiller

C    It used to give 'D' cystitis

               Smokes all his own fish

B    right

       G    why is Everything Swedish so much better

C    All that um, Citrus

D    Are you talking about me having cystitis

G    like what's that Concept? Hygge?

C    The margaritas

F    Oh I Love Hygge

E    amazing

       D    the Most horrific cystis

C    Have one 'B' - drink up.

B    .

Thanks.

A    So so so - let me - let's properly - because - so, this is 'C' and 'D' - This is their lovely home

D    Welcome

C    And 'E's home

E    Not really

A    What

E    I'm just staying here for a bit

A    What the fuck are you on about

E    Oh God, long story - NAME1 broke up with / me

F    / How do you not / Know that

A    / Fuck off - how Do I not know that I'm / so sorry

I    / Uhhhh cos you're a shit friend love / you're really not, like Present

E    / Oh God it was - honestly - it was a long time coming. Work and Life and. Oh God, we just disagreed on Everything / and

G    / NAME1 is a dick

H    I really liked NAME1

G   That is so / unhelpful

E   / No no no it's not - I really / liked NAME1

H   / I just thought he had such an extraordinary Spirit. / You know?

G   extraordinary spirit

E   / it's fine - we were. Oh God, we were Great for like.

H   yeah?

     Eight years

G   really?

B   wow

H   yeah

E   Yeah. I mean. Great guy to. Play Scrabble with? Climb a hill with?

E   The Sex got Awful

A   What kind of Awful

G   Abusive awful?

I   Good Abusive Awful or Bad Abusive / awful

C   'B' eat up by the way

H   You're so outrageous

E   UnAbusive awful - so - so - we're selling the house and the flat / and everything and

     this is just how we talk

A   / Oh fuck man

B   right

E   And these sweet people are taking me in

A   You're selling the Berlin flat

E    Fraid so

A    Oh my god I'm going to Cry

            I    I'm gonna order something do you Mind

G    Who guessed 8.30 who had her crying by 8.30

C    Order something

D    she means coke

C    oh

            G    you were so offended you're so delicate

F    were you so offended

H    'C' is an incredible cook

B    right

H    It would be deeply offensive if 'I' was actually ordering takeaway food or something

B    sure, I, yeah, I understand

H    but it's Drugs, she's actually Ordering / drugs

B    / right

A    They had The most incredible flat in Kreuzberg and we had Such amazing nights there. Fucker. I was going to take 'B'

B    excuse me?

A    I mean. Profoundly sorry about your enormous break up of course but. The Berlin / flat

E   / I know I know - I knew you'd be devastated

A   Devastated is not even the word how long have you Been / here

E   / Three months?

A   I'm such a bad friend

C   We love having her here

D   Makes work so much easier - 'E' has been working with us

A   What?

C   In the um pub - I think you guys have been, I just wasn't there

A   'C' runs that pub that we went to a few weeks ago

B   oh right

    It was lovely. Congratulations.

    I don't / I don't think I Want to go to Berlin

A   / She owns the pub - and three others - why are you Working there

B   I don't want to go to / Berlin

E   / I'm just doing some shifts - I took some time off work

A   'E' is a detective

I   You're a cunt

G   a massive cunt

B     oh

H     An Amazing detective

A     Why the fuck are you working in a Pub

D     What's wrong with working in / a Pub

F     / Massive fucking burn

G     Woooooaaaaah

A     Absolutely nothing obviously

E     I just wanted to

D     The fuck is wrong with pub work you shit

A     You don't Work in a pub you Run Four Pubs you Cannot get offended

E     I just wanted to do something that didn't involve extreme levels of fucking violence and trauma just for a / few weeks

F     / I Hear That

G     It was quite funny sometimes though wasn't it

E     I mean, not really? No, not / what I'd call a funny job

G     / Yeah it was - what about ummm that female flasher

F     Oh my God yes, What did she even flash

E     Her vagina and her breasts

H     You don't mean vagina

E   I absolutely do

H   You mean her vulva and her pubis

F   Uhhhh

E   The Pubis is the Bone, she wasn't showing her Bone, I couldn't see her Bone

C   Can everyone try the fattoush please

D   It's delicious

H   Okay but she wasn't flashing her vagina, she wasn't flashing her Internal organ she was flashing the labia / and the pubic Region

E   / Yeah, probably. That was yeah

F   So much easier to be a male flasher - it's all just fucking There

H   Yes

G   And makes more psychological sense - look what I've got whereas this woman. Maybe she was trying to Display her Mystery? You know?

     Reveal that she Contains, Holds so / much Power

B   / is that a useful way to Talk about the / Female body

E   / I mean. It didn't read that way when we took her statement for the fifteenth time but it's a nice story    A   you're so great

                                                                                               B   What?

D   I mean, it sounds quite funny though - in terms of Crimes

                                                                                                        A   you're just

E   I mean not really, it was just really fucking sad

D   Who was she flashing                  really fucking great

E   Old people mostly             B .

G   That Is really sad             right

F   the fattoush is delicious 'C'

A   Are you going Back? To work?      C   Oh good

E   Maybe. Yeah? I dunno.

C   I mean. It's been good hasn't it? All living together

E   Amazing

D   We're completely insufferable with it - we wake up and do yoga together

E   I used to teach yoga

B   wow.

G   I'm going to vomit in your labneh

*L has entered. L has a bicycle helmet on and a deliveroo (or similar) jacket. No one notices L for a moment.*

F   A detective cum chef cum yoga teacher, how fucking Extraordinary / are you

H   / Have you tried the labneh 'B'

B   um

H    It's incredible

B    what / is labneh

D    / So, yeah, yoga and mindfulness and we eat altogether and we're going on Holiday together

C    It's just a strained yoghurt

D    .

    What is

C    Labneh.

D    And you're just announcing that Why

C    'B' asked

D    Oh right - God sorry, I thought you'd just entirely / lost your mind

B    / I've not had it - sorry I

D    Just shouting about Strained yoghurt / for literally no reason

F    / Don't worry - all of my life's firsts have happened around this table - it's perfectly normal to not know what the fuck labneh / is

C    / you have it with flatbreads, it's delicious

A    Try it

L    um

B    I

C    Try it

B    Well I

C    Just try it.

B

Lovely. Thanks.

A    Isn't it incredible.

B    Mm. Really amazing. Thank you.

A    Have some / more

B    / I will. Thank you - hi? Sorry there's a woman standing in your -

D    Oh my God

L    Hi - sorry

C    Fuck        F    Jesus Christ

D    Um            Scared the crap out of me

L    Hi I'm sorry

I    I love it when people wear bike helmets and they're absolutely nowhere near a bike

C     Sorry, can we help you?

I     There is literally nothing funnier

E     You can't just walk into someone's house

L     Yeah, sorry           D    who the fuck are you

G     Fucking yes - get all cop on her ass

L     Your door was Wide open

C     That doesn't matter - that's besides the

D     Fuck's sake 'A' - learn to close a fucking / door

A     / It wasn't us!

I     It just looks like you're incredibly safety conscious as a person

F     my heart / is Still pounding

I     / Like, you're scared of bumping into a wall or a door, or, like, a fucking Pillow / falling on you

B     / I think she's here to deliver something?

C

C     Do you know her?

B     Excuse me? Why would I know / her?

465

C You're talking like you Know her

D yeah, I thought maybe you Knew her

L and like, the Integrity of the company

E Don't even joke about it

L / I don't know her - I don't know that / woman

B no / I just

C Why would I know her?

C / (to I) Is she for you? Is this your drugs person?

L what

I Deliveroo does not deliver drugs

L yeah I'm not

I That would be fucking sweet, but they do not yet provide / that service

L / Yeah, no, I'm not delivering drugs - can you Not say stuff like that cos I / actually have a job to

I / Can you even Imagine

C Well I didn't fucking order anything - as if I would order / food

G / Busted - you didn't make Any of this

C This is really fucking offensive - you've got the wrong house

L 'C FULLNAME', ADDRESS

C .

G Fucking busted!

L    I've got, like, four cases of wine out there.

C    Ohhhhhhh.

L    Yeah. Right. Yep.

     I totally forgot I'd

L    Yeah, you put in the order, like, forty minutes ago?

D    You were quite slow then

C    I completely forgot - sorry

                                            G    How do you forget about Four cases of wine

L    I rang the bell.

                                            I    mmmm

C    Oh.

                                            G    that is a Lot of wine to like casually order

L    And then I felt a bit faint. Cos I'm on a bike. Not a motorbike. And you ordered, like, four cases. So. I thought I should just come in. And then

     you were talking about yoghurt for ages. And then I just felt like oh God, can no one even See me, like am I actually Here or not and so I didn't

     really know what to do, but your cases of wine are just in the, like, porch if that's okay.

B    Your head is bleeding.

L    Is it? Yeah. I fell over. Crashed into your wall.

D    Oh Jesus - did you hit any tiles

C    Fuck's sake 'D'

D    no, it's just, they were handmade in Portugal and I had to make Two trips, specifically to -

B    do you need some water        G    You're a twat

L    No, I should go, I've got a shit ton of orders. I just needed to sort of Lean against something. For a second.

C    d'you want to come in

L    no I

D    come in even further than she already has

L    Yeah, no, I need to get back to        G    you're being a massive twat

C    Course

B    Do you need someone to look at your head

L    Are any of you qualified to look at my head

I'm gonna get going then. Thanks.

I'd like to really reiterate that I don't sell drugs. I'd like to make that very clear. That's not why I'm in your property. Okay. Thanks. Thanks for.

Yeah.

*L leaves, almost falling over as she goes.*

A    I can't believe you forgot you ordered / Four cases of wine

C    / I know I know

D    She was Weird, wasn't there something / weird

H    / Really strange energy

E    But like the talking about the Company so much

D    Right?

H    There's a doc in that, riiiight

F    I mean, not my Thing, / but absoLutely

G    / Anyway - so I'm 'G' - I live three doors down

B    I

C    Can someone grab the wine / and make sure the door is shut

I    / sure sure sure. I'll check if she left any drugs

G    I'm a therapist

F    surprising, right

G    if we're doing our jobs - we seem to be doing our Jobs?

D    I didn't do my job


G    do you have a Problem

I    like a compulsive ordering problem

B    I think she'd hurt her head

F    Like she'd been Bugged or

H    really?

H    she didn't leave drugs

I    But she was SO protesty about it

H    Nah

E    I only / did my job because

C    / we only did our jobs because it Made Sense in the / context of the conversation

E    / Exactly

C    You sound Mad

E    Announcing you're a therapist

G    Most of us Are mad

F    That's such a boring therapist joke, you can do better / than that

G    / I know, it was just / there, I just took it you know

B    / D'you think that woman was alright

H    I'm 'H' - we met - I introduced / myself

B    / Yes, yes hi

D    / I'm an Architect

F    You can't just Announce that why is everyone Announcing

H    I'm a HeadTeacher / at a local school

D    / We're doing Jobs - we're Clearly doing jobs

G    I work in institutions now, mostly, though I also see some private clients

I    So, like, methinks you Do protest too much

F    I know, I just Know that you're funnier than the 'All Therapists Are Mad' joke, you know, I really believe in your / humour

G    / I appreciate that

D    I designed this Whole house

H    She's the best

I    She is - I tried to see her in disguise once

G    It's unethical

B    yes sure that's

I    I really did - I really turned up on her doorstep in a fucking wig

B    right

I    I'm not fucking lying I did that, I had huge dark glasses on and a shit ton of make up

B    right

I    That happened

D    No one thinks you're making it up 'I' you don't have to convince us

E    'G' told us all about it at the time

F    I just Fundamentally disagree with that way of introducing yourself, don't you, 'B'

B    I

F    I'm 'F'. I like running and drinking and I'm not talking about my fucking job

D    What are you doing

F    I run really fucking hard because I drink really fucking hard, but I drink really fucking hard because I run so fucking hard, do you see

D    Seriously, what are you

F    I am Telling 'B' about myself. That was Specifically requested in the Email

I    Oh The FUCKING EMAIL

F    'Tell her - better yet, Show her - what brilliant and funny and great people you are and how you're such Good Friends to me'

A    Okay okay

E    'Allow Your Personalities - your Dynamic Personalities - to Shine through'

F    Maybe I could show you my running do you feel like our Dynamic Personalities are Shining through 'B'

B    did you really send that?

*F starts running laps of the table. She shouts while she runs. Every so often she stops to take a drink.*

F    Do you see?

B    That's           H   Isn't she hysterical

A    Are you okay are you having a fucking great time

B    I'm

I'm confused         F   I fucking love running

I    You look amazing doing it

F    I know

I    Like, I can see your abs, I swear I can see your abs

F    I know

A    'F' is Famous - That is why she is not talking / about her job

F    / I'm not famous - I'm 100% not famous        B    Oh right wow

E    She's so famous

F    I'm really not

D    She always does this and then we say her name and everyone is completely bowled over

B    Right

G    She's won three BAFTAs

B    Oh great. Congratulations

F    This is really

D    'F FULLNAME'

B    .

B    Right. Yes. I see.

*F stops running. Drinks.*

F    See. Run Hard, Drink Hard. Fuck jobs.

G  You have absolutely no idea who she is do you

B  I'm sorry I'm not really

I  That's fucking hilarious

B  I don't. / I don't watch the BAFTAs

F  / Oh my God, you don't please - it's not          E  Eeeesh

A  She makes the most incredible documentaries          G  so awkward

C  We're going to eat soon          E  'I don't watch the BAFTAs'

G  Definitely already eating    E  Smells so good 'C'          B  Can I help with anything    I  No one watches the fucking

F  It's really not a big deal          C  God, no          BAFTAs

H  It really is though. She makes Very important work.

B  Right

H  It's very Dynamic. Very Authored. Full of movement. Aesthetically engaged.

F  so sweet

H  Are you not, like, Into documentaries or current affairs or the news or anything?

B  .

B  Yeah. No. I am. I just haven't / heard of her

G    / We have been So Excited to meet you 'B'.

B    Right

G    Like, Giddy

A    Don't scare her                                  B    Giddy? That's a

D    We've never seen 'A' so happy

F    It's true

D    And she doesn't really have any family left, so we're like. Family. You know?

G    And there was a difficult paternal relationship so. It's been really vital to model a new, Healthy kind of family for 'A'.

H    She's had some really difficult relationships

A    Maybe don't go there

G    There have been some Deeply unhealthy ones

A    Could we keep it sexier

G    Not Abusive but. Damaging and Self Sabotaging and Co-Dependent

A    Yeah, I want this woman to find me Attractive

G    But she's done an awful lot of work on herself

D    She's really been seeking something Steady

G  That's such a good word 'D'

D  Thank you.

H  And you're a teacher

B

   Yes.

   Yep.

H  Because I'm a headteacher.

B

   Yep. Yes.

   Congratulations

C  *(carrying dishes of food)* Okaaaaaay so

A  That smells Incredible    E  watch your backs

C  just going to make a little room    D  oh wow

A  How do you do it 'C'

F  Every Single Time

E  She's been Non Stop all day

H  You have Excelled yourself    F  this looks

G  oh my god    So Good

H  so impressive

C   'B' do you eat everything

G   How do we know none of this is Deliveroo

C   Fuck off please

A   She's so sweet

E   I know

A   Feeding us all like this / we're so lucky

C   / Is there anything you don't eat

B   Ummmm. No? No, I eat pretty / much everything

A   / She's not fussy - as if I'd bring someone fussy / to your house

D   / We'd have to kill you if you did

H   They're so passionate about food, it's really a pleasure - I feel like I get an Education every time I come here

C   What does pretty much mean

D   Huh

C   Pretty much, 'B' you said pretty much everything - what don't you eat

B   Um

G   You sound a tiny bit like you're interrogating her

C   I do not, no I don't, that's not - no - the Opposite, I'm trying to / I'm

G  / WHAT DON'T YOU EAT

F  TELL US WHAT THE FUCK IT IS THAT YOU DON'T EAT

C  that is not

E  she's just being a good Host

C  I'm just trying to Ascertain What it is She doesn't eat

F  She

C  What it is You don't eat

B  I um - I really Do eat most / things

C  / sure sure sure but can you Name some of the things that you Do Not Eat

B  Um. Well.

D  Course - let anyone you Like in obviously

    Our home is Your home

H  I love that - it's like your Mantra

D  Yeah

H  Like, your House Motto

D  Yeah

H  Like, you should get that Engraved above the

I  'J's here, can I let her in

F  What Is this one

E  It's a spiced lamb sort of kofta thing

F  Woooow

G  That Smells amazing

B  I guess I don't Love cauliflower?

C  .

E  That's fine - there's just a Bit of cauliflower in that one

B    right

E    With tahini and uh lemon    D    door or um or on a Sign

A           C    So you can just avoid that one and    H    Aesthetically, that sounds Horrific

B    sounds incredible    really?

B    I mean, I Eat it - I can eat it I

C    Fuck no, you're not to do Polite eating of Anything in this house

B    Or flour I don't eat flour or dairy.

C    .

B    I'm kidding. That was a

C    oh my god

B    a joke

F    Your face

G    Ha    E    that's great

A    Isn't she funny? Isn't she fucking glorious

B    I eat dairy and flour really happily

C    thank fuck

D    What's this one

E   It's green beans and some spices and

C   So just help yourself - and have it with the flatbreads and the yoghurt and the pomegranate dip / and     D   Yum

H   / Incredible

I   This is 'J' everyone - she'll just be here for a second

D   Hi 'J'

J   How's it going

I   And this is - sorry, I didn't catch your

K   'K'

I   Great, yes - 'K', this is.

J's friend? J's. Companion. Or. Like. Associate? Partner? Like. Mate? 'K'.

K   Hi.

G   Great

C   Hi

H   Great to meet you both

I   They're just gonna hang out here while I

F   Ideal

I    Just while I do money stuff

J    That food looks incredible

            C    D'you want to pull up a chair

I    the fuck is my purse

G    You're such a fucking feeder

J    no no, we're good - work is

C    Course

J    Nuts tonight - Thursday is the new Friday

E    Sure

H    I love that

    'Thursday is the new Friday' that's great

A    what's this one

C    you can have a flatbread whilst you wait

J    If you're sure

            J    this looks great thank you

C    She'll be ages

C    'K' - please

K    No thanks. I've got dinner reservations in a bit. That Moroccan restaurant in the / square

C    / That place is so great

K    so I'm just gonna Stand over here if that's okay.

G    Like a bodyguard or

K    If you like. You have a great space here. Great ambience.

D    Thank you so much. I designed it myself.

K    I can tell. It really has that homebuilt feel. It's fantastically inviting.

A    How's the film going 'F'

F    this is inCredible - yeah good - thanks

A    'F' is making this amazing doc about the um

F    It's about the Me Too movement

B    The sorry, the what?

F    .

B    The um. The movement - the Me Too Movement

B    the what movement

F    Me Too.

B    .

D    thanks so much

K    you're so welcome

F

Me Too

As in.

MeToo.

As in.

Am I [going nuts]

the Hashtag Me Too movement - it was a

G   Huge deal

B   right            E   Everywhere

H   She's right, it was Everywhere       C   Major

D   It still Is everywhere

H   She's right

J   It was huge            E   It's like, the most important event of the last

K   It Is huge

D   We're still having conversations about it at work - Constantly - you know? Building into the fabric of how we run our company

G          Huge

F    It was about.

It was triggered by

The sort of - these revelations. The. Hollywood casting couch. Sexual assault.

B    .

right.

A    Isn't it extraordinary? It's like she lives under a rock.

F    And then. This Global movement. Women everywhere. Telling their stories. Owning their pain.

I can't believe you haven't Heard of it - it's been Life Changing.

G    It's Mad

B    Wow. This is delicious by the way.

Life changing.  Wow.

A    Are you eating the cauliflower

B    I want to be polite - it's very / edible

C    / Oh my God stop it, stop eating it

B    And you said Global movement? Like. Everywhere?

F    Everywhere

C Can you just Stop eating the fucking cauliflower please

B Like. Literally Global. Huge change happening in villages in France and Syria and Myanmar, that's extraordinary.

F Yeah. Yeah. I mean, it's happening to varying degrees in different places but it's Global, it feels Global

B Feels

F Yes

B It Feels global To You or it Is global, factually?

F .

  It's been Enormous. It's been a Seismic shift. It's causing real change.

B It's causing real change on the Hollywood Casting Couch.

F Everywhere.

  To a degree.

  Everywhere.

K I think we've even noticed the impact in our line of work you know

J For sure       H That is Fascinating

B In the drug dealing industry you've noticed the impact of Me Too

K For sure absolutely     E wow

J   No doubt

B   In what way exactly

J   I mean it's hard to Quantify but you can just Tell - the conversations that we're all having - you can just Tell

B   The Conversations

F   I mean, it's been a Revolution

J   Yes absolutely

B   Right

K   It's a real shift

G   It really has

B   A revolution

A   that's amazing

F   yes exactly

B   On Twitter

F   .

    Everywhere.

A   Isn't she extraordinary?

G   are you On Twitter

B   No I'm not On Twitter

H   'T' works for Twitter

J    She's essentially responsible for the increased character allowance

F    The revolution Began on Twitter but it's fucking everywhere

B    The overthrow or repudiation and then the thorough replacement of an established government or system by the people governed.

    Real, profound, structural, lasting, permanent change for absolutely everybody - from the leaders of countries, Presidents, Prime Ministers,

    down to the voiceless, those in society who lack / power and agency

H    / how far off are you from finishing / the film

F    / uuummmmm / like

B    / Revolution. Based around a / movement

A    / are you okay / or

F    / maybe four / more weeks of filming

B    / fine - based around a Movement / called Me Too

A    / d'you want a Drink / or something like

F    / and then the edit and / you know

G    / so intense

B    one that is built / around the importance of the individual

K    / sounds like a fascinating project

A    you should definitely have / a drink

B    / which is not normally how revolutions occur - so that's

F    I mean I'm normally - I do a lot of stuff in um in prisons and War Zones

B    Stuff?

F    Yeah

B    You Do a lot of Stuff in prisons and war zones?

That sounds

A    Isn't she amazing

Really

J    what a fascinating group of people you are

F    Make films.

B    Right

F    That's. I've made two films In a war zone - from the Middle of a war zone - I'm just explaining my Credentials to you, my Experience

H    Extraordinary

F    This has been like nothing else. It's a really Profound and deeply important moment - Real Change, Real Lasting Change

B    Sure.

It sounds incredible.

F    It is. It was. It Is.

B    I was just trying to understand / the Specifics. The Global. The Everyone. Revolution. Movements attract hyperbole.

F    / It's been really incredible

E    It's so amazing you're doing it.                    J    It sounds really inspiring

H    Do the girls at your school not talk about it?

B    The girls?

H    Sorry. The school I'm head of is a Girls School

D    Such a good school

G    My kids both went there

J    What's the name

H    SCHOOLNAME

K    Nice school

J    Oh my niece goes there

H    Oh.

     That's.

     What's her name

J    I mean I can't really Disclose that it's

H    Sure

J    Confidentiality

H    Confidentiality

J    Because of my job

B    Because you're here to sell drugs

J    yeah, I mean. yeah. That's it.

B    No, the kids at my school don't talk about the Hashtag Me Too Movement, no. / Not really. No.

E    / So do you guys, like work together or

J    yeah

E    That's for like protection or

K    You're a cop aren't you

E    I

K    You talk like a cop

E    I work in a pub

K    Yeah, but you're a cop in your heart right

E     That's funny

J     She's just coming with me for tonight

F     Right

J     I'm going on holiday next week so she's doing my rounds

H     Oh wow

G     Holiday cover

J     Exactly

C     Such a smart idea

J     Yeah. I mean, so much business round here, I don't want to let anyone down - she covered my maternity / last year

C     / Sure sure

I     So sorry - I had to take a call - here is this good

J     Yeah

      Good - and this is yours

I     Perfect

*'I' sets about doing a line immediately*

C     Finish your food 'J' you're more than welcome

J     I'd love to, but I have A Lot of people waiting

H    And I bet most of them won't offer you labneh and flatbread

J    No, I mean.

     That's.

     Most of them will to be honest. Some variant on.

     Nice neighbourhood.

H    Sure

E    That's great

J    Have you got enough

A    We're all set, thanks

K    Have a great night guys

D    Thanks 'J'

I    Thanks a million

C    Nice to meet you

*J and K have gone. More people do lines of coke from here.*

I    Aren't they so great? 'J' is such a fascinating / person

A    / Of course You think she's great, you press a button and she turns up with drugs

I    I mean, I Pay her. I Pay her really well it's not like she Gives it to me - can you imagine if she just / Gave it to me

B    / (to C and D) How did you guys meet?

C    .

     Us?

D    We met doing volunteer work

A                                                                    E    They're a dream couple

A    They're not joking

B    Wow

C    We were in Bolivia

B    Probably where your drugs come from

D    Working in an orphanage

C    I'd just got out of this Twelve Year relationship with this

A    Oh my God, psycho                          E    NAME4

F    Crazy fucking NAME4

C    And wanted to just go and Be somewhere completely different and get out of myself.

B    Lucky orphans.

D    Lucky me.

C    It was the most extraordinary ten days of my life

B    Ten Days

D    Ten Perfect Days                                    C    Life changing

B    And. Presumably life changing for the kids too. Ten days. For those orphans.

F    It's such a headache having such perfect friends

H    Completely impossible to start a relationship when you witness These Two all the time

A    Speak for yourself

B    I um had these friends who met when they were doing this build a well thing in um in Kenya

G    Wow

B    And they said that they Realised on the last day that in the night, the locals, the villagers, were coming down to where they had been building

     this Well, and they were Rebuilding it. Because they - these people I know - and the whole volunteer team - obviously can't build a fucking

     well, they've not got the necessary building skills. So, because the locals didn't want to Offend the volunteers, they would come and rebuild it

     Properly in the middle of the night

G    right

I    that's funny

H    I was thinking about / your wedding the other day

B    / so that on the last day all the English tourists got a really lovely Warm feeling / of of having Helped

C    / about Our wedding?

H    yeah        E      such a great day      D     sweet

B    and could go Home and feel really / excellent about themselves

H    / just, like the dancing and the - God, your / dogs

G    / oh your dogs

B    but actually, all that had happened was - they had Paid a charity to fly them over and let them do skilled work

A    and the speeches

F    oh my God the speeches

D    my Dad      C     your Dad

B    that they were not Qualified for - for free - in a / in a community

G    / and wasn't there a magician? / why did you have a magician

E    / that magician was groping literally everybody      B    where actually the locals might really benefit from

I    of course he was groping everybody, everyone knows that magician is a code      from Paid Work and that. I just.

      job for assaulter -

C     And we know how you two met, of course.

B     Oh.

A     I told them.

D     Several times

B     I mean it's not that interesting, I'm surprised it's worthy of telling more than once

G     It's sort of extraordinary

B

G     We met at a wedding?

D     And then fucked round the back of the marquee?

H     That certainly Sounds extraordinary to me

G     Mind Blowing

A     Okay

G     She said Mind Blowing A Lot

A     I tell them everything

B     right

A    I was very excited

F    Sounded like you both were

D    We were very excited for her

G    Sounds like you Wanked over it

D    I kind of did – we kind of did, don't you / remember

F    / We've all received fairly Graphic and Detailed descriptions of your vagina

A    I mean. I'm just a massive fan.

G    I feel like I could draw it

D    I'd definitely know it if I saw it.

B    .

      'A'

.  A    It is So Nice to be here with all of you guys

F    Ahhhh

A    I feel So Lucky

E    Here we go

A    No, I do. To be here with all of my Incredible friends

C    ahhhh

A    And This woman

This Incredible woman

Who has Changed my life.

D    Sweet.

B    Are you Crying

D    Of Course she's crying

E    She loves a good cry

H    I think it's Moving

I do, I think it's really moving how close to your Emotions you are

I    D'you want some of this

F    Great idea, get her even closer to her emotions

C    It's Good to cry. It's Healthy

D    Particularly in a job where she has to be so Serious all the time

A    Thank you

B    Are you really Crying?

F    It's not a Gathering of us all if 'A' doesn't bawl her eyes out

E    You must have seen some version of this

B    Um. No? Genuinely, no? I feel like I'm meeting an entirely different / unfuckable person tonight?

A    / I'm just really tired

D    Unfuckable? Did she just?

B    Your face is really wet

I    that's hilarious

A    I have this Case

D    The uh the husband killer one

C    They're all husband killer ones

H    That's her speciality

A    It's not my Speciality it's just

E    It's definitely what you're Drawn to

D    You are Absolutely making a name for yourself as

C    For sure

A    I mean it's my - it's what I'm passionate about, what I give a Shit about it's

I    Was there ever any crossover - did you Arrest people she did then Defended

E    Uhhhh / Yeah

A    / Yeah - Once or

E    Twice yeah it was

A    Fine it was

E    Fine - and normally, fucking hell, normally when she showed up it was Relief from my end

H    right

E    Cos they're not fucking Career criminals

F    Obviously

E    it's not like it's Myra Hindley ever week

I    Myra Hindley was fucking Hot / right

A    / Myra Hindley was vulnerable and manipulated

B    sorry what

I    She was a bit though

B    no the bit about her being / vulnerable - what?

E    / So whenever 'A' showed up it was like, okay, great, here is Evidence that this woman who is obviously in need of Help is going to Get Help

*M enters. M is a child. The others don't pay much attention to her, apart from B who seems transfixed.*

M    Can I have some water.

D    Help yourself sweetheart

I   D'you want some coke

M   No thank you

I   I'm fucking around

M   Hello 'I', nice to see you

F   Of course not

A   They're not All husband killers by the way

B   (to M) Hi.

F   It's much more complex than that

H   'F' did a documentary about prisons

B   right. yes. she said. Stuff in war zones and prisons

F   About women's prisons specifically

B   right

F   Most of my work has a female angle

B   right.

M   Mum

C   Yes

D   Yes

M   Can I eat some of this

B   and sorry - what's a female angle

C   Course you can sweetheart

F   Well. I'm a woman

B   yes

F   And my work centres on women

B   yes

F   And of course, God, prisons aren't full of husband killers - or killers of any kind

E   It's just women on this rotation

H   Absolutely      G   Mmmm

F   Exactly - of repeat offences - shoplifting, drug possession, soliciting - not crimes where anyone is really At risk

B   The person they're stealing from might dispute that     E   But, so This case

A   She's just. God, she's just Got to me so much more than she Should have done.

M   Is this fish?

D   Which one sweetheart

M   This one in the blue bowl

C   Yes love - have the chicken, you'll like the chicken

G   What is it / about this one - this Case

A   / Oh I mean I just don't even know - it's not like it's

It's no Different from the rest, it's. Usual shit. Cycle of abusive partners. Horrific childhood - I mean Really horrific - Unimaginable horrific -

B   (*to M*) How old are you?

C   She's (actual age of actor playing M)

B   Oh

A   rape, violent boyfriends, drug addiction

F   Classic

M   I'm going to take this upstairs now

D   Okay petal

H   Night night sweet 'M'        G   Night love        D   Night darling        C   Do you need anything        A   Night

M   I'm fine thanks

B   Nice to meet you

M   You too

*M leaves*

A   I mean her Mother was a prostitute and used to just Take her with her from when she was about Nine so

D    Jeeeesus

E    Fuck Off man

A    But this is - this is Standard, so. Fuck knows why I'm so

C    It's upsetting

A    Yeah. Yes. It is. Yes.

And she'll get convicted.

For fucking ages.

It was self defence it's not even - it's Boring how Obvious that is to anyone who could just take a fucking look

F    Obviously

A    But.

She's a fucking horrible defendant.

G    In what way

A    Surly.

I    Good word.

A    Rude. Bored. She falls asleep. Catatonic. Unengaged. Smiles at the Worst fucking moments and then Loses her shit if she thinks someone looks

at her the wrong way

C    Why isn't she on shitloads of medication

A    I mean she is. She is.

She's Out of it.

And.

She is Profoundly Sad.

And has been

Entirely let down by Absolutely Everybody for her whole life.

The amount of times she must have witnessed someone give up on her.

Someone Paid To Fuck Her when she was Nine. And her Mum Took the money. Put her in that position. Her Mum. Her fucking Mum. My

Mum held my Hand until I fell asleep when I was Nine because I was still scared of monsters - her Mum rented out her child's Vagina so she

could put bigger volumes of heroin in her eyeballs - like of Course she is selecting violent boyfriends and then beating them to death and of

Course I'm a fucking lawyer - like what's the Point, what are we all Doing, why is the world so Extraordinarily Fucked - she Hammered and

Stabbed and Kicked him to death with her Kids in the room and I want to Scream well of course she fucking did, we're all to blame, she had no

Choice - she had no fucking Choice

B    Can I just use your bathroom?

C

      Sure. Down the hall. On your left.

E    Or there's a huge one upstairs.

B    A huge loo?

E    A huge bathroom. It's lovely. Covered in photos. Just. If you prefer a more

F    Scenic / pee

    / Do not say scenic pee

B    .

    Right.

    Thanks.

    *She leaves.*

C    I'm gonna grab pudding.

    *More people take more drugs.*    G    Oh God I'm so ready for pudding

E    D'you need a hand

C    I'm fine - was there not enough / food

G    / No no no - I just Love your pudding

C    Cos there's more of everything / I can get you Anything

G    / nonononono

F   So. 'B' is

A   Yeah

F   I mean

A   Isn't she

G   I don't think I've ever

H   She's certainly

A   I know

D   She's kind of

A   I am so in love with her.

D   .

    Yeah.

H   Great.

E   That's wonderful.

G   Really great.

F   .

    Yes. She's fascinating.

A   Isn't she?

    She wants kids

E   Wow.

    That is.

    Information

    With you? As in

G   It's really hard. To have kids - I know that's really boring - but it just fucking is, they can be fucking horrible

A   I just think it could be amazing

G   I know it's such a cliche to say that - it's so boring, but they really can fuck everything up

A   I just. I think she's like. Earth. You know.

H   Mmmmm

I   I'm making the conscious choice not to reproduce due to climate change

G   I think that's a really fucking sensible idea

I   I mean I know you think it's cos I'm fucking mad

E   And because you hate children

I    I do hate children

G    Right

I    But I actually fundamentally am basing my decision on the fact that the planet is fucked

B    (entering) That's really noble of you.

     You've all been friends for such a long time.

D    Yeah. Yeah, we have.

B    Those photos

H    Amazing aren't they

B    You've done everything together

G    Yeah

B    Just like non stop women's marches and villa holidays and skiing trips and dinners and ironic karaoke nights

F    Fucking hell we sound like cunts.

B

C    This is a clafoutis everyone. And some ice creams. Just. Dig In.

G    Amazing    H    Thank you So much    F    Smells incredible    D    You're such a Goddess

E    I didn't even notice you cook this

C    Clafoutis is a piece of piss - 'B' have you got a drink

B    I'm fine

C    Have some clafoutis

B    I think I'd rather stick a fork in my fucking eye than have any clafoutis but thanks.

C    .

B    I just pissed on your daughter, by the way. On 'M'.

     Just now.

     I just pissed on her.

C    .

     Excuse me?

D    Are you serious? Is she serious - why are you grinning

A    I can't help it - your face - she's not serious

B    No no no - I Am - I did do that.

E    .

     The fuck?

B    She was asleep - she was fast asleep, but I guess I might have woken her up when I stepped Up onto the bed and sort of Straddled her and then

pissed all over her - I guess she might have woken / up

D    are you Serious 'B'

B    Yeah. I pissed all over your child.

A    .

C    She's fucking about

C    I'm not sure I get it

F    Oh my God                                    G    Fucking hell

D    Okay. She's fucking weird. I've been Nice, but This one, 'A'? This is the one?

B    My Mum used to piss on me. When I was a kid and she'd come back drunk - she'd piss on me - not by Accident, not because she Mistook me

for a toilet, but because she Could and because she was Mean and because she was Abusive and so then when I came in here and saw how

much you Have and how Life is So Full and Easy for you - the only things that went through my tiny brain were FUCK ME I'm fucking

envious of everything these people have And I can't control my bladder on account of my horrific / childhood experience

D    / Is she fucking with us

E    She's definitely fucking with us              F    The fuck?

A    Okay. Okay okay okay I                        G    Am I

B    Yeah I fucking pissed Everywhere

F    no, sorry, what the Fuck

E    That is a Crime, that is a criminal Act

B    So's all that coke that's falling out of your nose

E    Not the same thing

B    You're right - my piss hasn't fucking been responsible for anyone's death or the decimation of an entire community and economy

F    that is So Boring

B    My piss was a necessary bodily function that Shit up your nose has just turned You into an even more boring and insufferable twat as far as I can tell

E    What the fuck

F    oh my God

I    I really like this one

B    You all act like Evil doesn't exist. You're all sitting in a ginormous fucking bleeding heart bubble of hypocrisy acting like Nobody should be held responsible for their actions yet feeding labneh to the drug dealer as though that doesn't Cost someone something

H    It doesn't exist

A    What

H    She said we are Acting like evil doesn't exist and it doesn't - I don't / believe it Does

B    / That is really fucking easy for you to say when you have Never encountered it

D    You don't know that - you don't Know us

B    yeah I fucking do

H    Should. Should someone go and Check on 'M'

C    Yes - yes of course I - 'D' can you go

D    Me

C    Yes - I

D    .

    Yes but. Yes but. Can You not say anything until I get back because this is fucking

A    I'm not Saying that someone who had an abusive childhood who Then goes onto commit a crime should be absolved from All responsibility

    because of their childhood 'B' - I'm just saying we should Talk about it

B    Except you don't fucking Talk about it - not Actually - not in depth, you don't Talk and Listen and Communicate

A    Pass the wine please - like, if you Did piss on their only child

B    Why does it matter more if it's their Only child

C    she didn't you didn't

A    If you Have done that, then hearing about your Mother urinating

B    Pissing

A    I'm being a Lawyer right now, Urinating on you as a child, would be really important evidence to hear because it Explains your actions. It's

Mitigating Circumstances - it stops you being a straightforward Nutjob or a / Psychopath or a

B    / Nutjob is legal terminology is it

A    Yes right now you absolute whackjob

C    It's certainly making me more forgiving of your Aloofness - like - Ah, it all makes sense

G    Always the Mother

C    Right? I mean - Politely Eat The Cauliflower please for Fuck's sake

B    I did! I fucking did politely eat the cauliflower and it was disgusting

D    (coming back in) She didn't piss on her

A    Of course she didn't piss on her

                                        B        of course I didn't piss on her

D    She's fast asleep

C    (to B) Thank you

F    Don't say Thank you that's Insane - don't Thank her for not pissing on your daughter

B    My Mother Did piss on me and I am fully capable of controlling my bladder - I am able to not Repeat her patterns of behaviour - I am able to

Choose not to hurt others, despite the fact that my Mother effectively Taught me to - I take Responsibility for my own actions, so you sitting

here surrounded by your Maize crisps and your fucking small plates of - what the fuck Is that by the way, it's Delicious but what Is it -

Sobbing for a woman who beat a man's brains out with a hammer all because her Mummy wasn't Nice to her is fucking Offensive to those of us who Try

C    Try

B    yes Try

F    You don't think we Try

B    No

F    Constantly

B    No

F    To Do Good - to Be Better - to Make a Fucking difference

B    No. Not with any depth or complexity or feeling. No. I don't think you do. I think you Say the right fucking things to one another. I think you Observe and Consume and Nourish yourselves with as much of the Awful as you can possibly stomach each day, in order to buy yourself the time and the life to do absolutely nothing of worth or meaning or good in the world. I think you will spend your whole lives making no change. Living in your bubbles. Patting one another on the back. Crying for people rather than condemning. Failing to either Listen or have a Complex conversation and Learn. I think you are making the world worse. Every single fucking day.

*She stands up. Maybe she stands on the table.*

Thank you so much for dinner.

I had a wonderful time.

*Maybe A kisses her.*